The Five-Faced Hindu God and My Tryst with Five Super Souls

Books Published by Allied Publishers for Dr. Siddhartha Ganguli

1. Live Happily, Work Happily - 2009
   3rd Reprint 2014
2. SUCCESS Can be Planned and Earned - 2010
   1st Reprint 2013
3. Greying Gracefully: Planning for Retirement and Old Age Happiness - 2011
4. Conscious Management - 2011
5. The Making of a Winning Child - 2012
6. Smart Leading and Parenting of Teenage Kids in the Digital Era - 2021
7. Music is Magic Music is Medicine: Impact of Music on Body, Brain, Mind & Soul - 2023
8. The Four Moons in the Human Body The Mysterious Tales of the Bauls of Bengal (Introducing 'BaulOlogy') - 2023
9. Love: A Good MedicineThe Saga of the Elixir of Life (Introducing 'LoveOlogy') - 2024
10. Goddess Kali God Thoughts Sri Sri Ramakrishna and A Few Slices of Sri Sri Ramakrishna's Soul (Introducing 'SoulOlogy') - 2024
11. The 'Real' Ramakrishna: As I Have Come to Know Him as Ramakrishna's Child *(Winner of the Golden Book Award 2025)* - 2024
12. The Third Eye The Mystery of Sri Sri Ramakrishna's Visions - 2024

The Five-Faced Hindu God and My Tryst with Five Super Souls

Siddhartha Ganguli, *PhD*

(Winner of the Golden Book Award 2025)

ALLIED PUBLISHERS PVT. LTD.

Noida • Mumbai • Kolkata • Chennai • Bangalore

ALLIED PUBLISHERS PRIVATE LIMITED

D-5, Sector-2, **Noida**–201 301
Ph. Nos.: 0120-4320295/2542557/4352866
E-mail: delhi.books@alliedpublishers.com

17 Chittaranjan Avenue, **Kolkata**–700072
Ph.: 033-22129618 • E-mail: cal.books@alliedpublishers.com

15 J.N. Heredia Marg, Ballard Estate, **Mumbai**–400001
Ph.: 022-42126969 • E-mail: mumbai.books@alliedpublishers.com

No. 25/10, Commander-in-Chief Road, Ethiraj Lane (Next to Post Office)
Egmore, **Chennai**–600008
Ph.: 044-28223938 • E-mail: chennai.books@alliedpublishers.com

P.B. No. 9932, No. 15, 3rd Floor (Next to Vijaya Bank), 5th Cross, Gandhinagar,
Karnataka, **Bangalore**–560009. Ph.: 080-41530285/22386239
E-mail: bngl.books@alliedpublishers.com

Website: www.alliedpublishers.com

ISBN: 978-93-89934-89-2

Front Cover Design:
Courtesy: Korean-Italian artist, Myunghwa Yoo su from Tuscany, Italy.

Published by Sunil Sachdev and printed by Ravi Sachdev
at Allied Publishers Pvt. Ltd., D-5, Sector-2, Noida–201 301

Dedication

To the Memory of
All the Five Super Souls
Covered in this Book

Foreword

Bridge. That is the commonplace but entirely apt metaphor Siddhartha Ganguli uses to describe the multifarious aim of this prolific author's latest book, *The Five-Faced Hindu God and My Tryst with Five Super Souls*. His bridge is five-fold: between science and Hinduism (but spirituality more generally); between Glasgow where he completed his post-graduate studies in bio-engineering and Kolkata where he lives and writes; between the five-headed Ganesha and the five super-souls he admires: James Watt, Adam Smith, Lord Kelvin, Sri Sri Ramakrishna and Sri Krishna Chaitanya Mahaprabhu; and most importantly between how we understand the universe now—chemical reactions, black holes, dark matter and dark energy—and how it was understood then—ecstatic and ascetic surrender of self, the dark god Krishna, and the dark goddess Kali. It's an ambitious undertaking and, in an age of growing religious fundamentalism on one hand and selfies and STEM (Science, Technology, Engineering and Math) on the other, a rather risky one, hoping to enlighten but courting skepticism.

I prefer to read Ganguli's slim book not as a finished bridge but instead as an engineer's, or bio-engineer's, sketches and notes for that bridge: not, that is, as a structure that will enable readers to cross quickly and safely from one side to the other, but rather as a set of provocations for those on either side—religious conservatism or scientific skepticism—who may, or will, feel themselves challenged by the points of contact the author proposes. In this regard Ganguli may be going one step further than did Swami Vivekananda who, during his own age of momentous scientific and technological advances, sought to adapt Hindu ideas to a western audience and did so with huge success, with his influence continuing to this day. Where Vivekananda began his 1893 address at the World Congress of Religions 'Sisters and brothers of America,' Ganguli addresses *Tryst* to conservative Hindus on one hand and scientists on the other, drawing parallels between the two, connecting, or attempting to connect, seemingly distant dots. Some of these connections strike even a postmodern skeptic like myself as surprisingly compelling, his discussions of, for example, Ramakrishna's devotion for the Goddess Kali in relation to dopamine hunger and the oxytocin effect.

Skeptical readers would do well to recall Colin Wilson's discussion of Ramakrishna, along with the poet Wiliam Blake and Society of Friends (Quakers) founder George Fox, as 'visionaries' whose views offered an alternative to the Western philosophic pessimism of Jean-Paul Sartre and others. In its own way Ganguli's *Tryst* is part of a recent movement towards this larger vision that is also evident in two aptly titled novels, Richard Powers' *The Overstory* and Anthony Doerr's *All the Light We Cannot See*. Even clearer, in my mind, as an American reader (a good postmodern skeptical one at that), are the similarities between *Tryst* and the mid-Nineteenth Century American Transcendentalists, who were deeply influenced by and drew on then recent translations of Hindu sacred writings to explore the relationship between science (especially technological progress) and spiritual improvement (in their cases outside formal eligions). This is especially evident in Ralph Waldo Emerson's essay on the Oversoul and more particularly in his earlier book, simply and provocatively titled Nature (1836), published, significantly enough, anonymously, as if it were not the individual author who wrote this slim volume but Nature itself--Nature Transcendentally considered, that is. For Emerson 'Nature' was not merely physical and other (as in the phrase 'go into nature' as if it were a National Park). It was not a place but a process of divesting oneself of 'all mean egotism' and becoming 'a transparent eyeball'—a seemingly cartoonish yet wonderfully evocative—or provocative—image. Indeed, Emerson's transparent eyeball accords well with the concluding scene of the 1954 Hindi biopic *Shri Chaitanya Mahaprabhu*, that Ganguli mentions in a note, in which a lap dissolve is used to show the title character (one of Ganguli's great souls) being drawn 'into the Dark God Jagannath's body—a *black hole* phenomenon.'

Often described as Emerson's disciple, Henry David Thoreau avoided Emersonian abstraction thanks to what critic F.O. Matthiessen called 'the check-rein of his senses' and arguably nowhere is this more compellingly evident than in a 1922-word passage in the the Spring chapter of Walden. Walking along a railroad embankment, Thoreau observes how the thawing sand resembles leaves, entire trees, then lungs and from there language itself in what we may think of as a mid-Nineteenth Century version of a Grand Unification Theory. His increasingly ecstatic language culminates this way: 'Thus it seemed that this one hillside illustrated the principle of all the principles of Nature. The Maker of this earth but patented a leaf. What Champollion will decipher this hieroglyphic for us, that we may turn over a new leaf at last?' Ganguli is attempting something similar, drawing on nearly two more centuries of science.

But I want to give the final word to the Walt Whitman, from his 1871 poem 'Passage to India. 'Singing my days, / Singing the great achievements of the present, / Singing the strong light works of engineers ....' For Whitman these remarkable engineering feats—the transcontinental railroad, the Suez Canal, the transatlantic cable—presaged not merely a global and literal passage to India; that, after all, had already long been accomplished, but instead a metaphorical and metaphysical one: a passage both back 'to primal thought' and ahead 'to more than India'. As I wrote earlier, Ganguli's trysts, or notes, as I prefer to call them, will provoke skepticism in some but connections in others who will see him as representing a new phase of a long tradition.

Robert Morace

1st March 2025

[Robert Morace, BA, MS, PhD is Distinguished Professor of English at Daemen College, Amherst, New York. He lectures on American Literature, Contemporary Fiction and Film. Author & Editor of several books, he has published a large number of articles. Winner of the 1996 Amy and Eric Burger Prize, he has taught in Warsaw, Poland and lectured in India.]

Contents

Molecules of Gratitude

It was so nice to relish the nostalgia of my *Alma Mater* – the University of Glasgow in Scotland, UK where I had spent a few glorious years of my youth as a research scholar. I could vividly remember the stone statues of Sir James Watt, Sir Adam Smith and Lord Kelvin when I was writing about them. I indeed feel grateful to their immortal souls.

I am grateful to my Bengali publisher Tapan Kumar Ghosh of Sahityasree, Mahatma Gandhi Road, Kolkata for arousing my interest to research deeply on the two *avatars* – Sri Sri Ramakrishna to start with and then later, on Sri Krishna Chaitanya Mahaprabhu.

I owe a lot to the published material: books, scientific papers, articles, video presentations and podcasts – both in Bengali and English that I had to refer to hunting for relevant data. My young journalist friend Subhajit Adhikari of the Bengali daily newspaper *Bartaman* was particularly helpful to discuss about the Vaishnava sect and Chaitanya Dev. For such discussions, I also thank the members of my fortnightly 'Spiritual Study Group' who meet at my place and participate with earnest interest. My novelist friend Amal Krishna Roy from North Bengal also deserves thanks as, although, he does not attend these fortnightly meetings, we have informal spiritual discussions regularly over phone and on WhatsApp.

I am indeed most thankful to Allied Publishers Pvt. Ltd., particularly Jagdish Singh of the Editorial Dept. and his team for undertaking the responsibility of processing my manuscript and make it see the light of day and also for its marketing and distribution through its own corporate and branch offices in India and also online worldwide.

My dear wife Utpala with whom I celebrated my 60th wedding anniversary in the month of January 2025 and our three kids –

Abhishek, Abhirup and Ishita have been taking keen interest in my research studies, writing and publishing work without any complaints that I do not give them enough time. My Personal Secretary Pervez Alam has, as usual, been extending his helping hand throughout this book project. Without his assistance, it would have been impossible for me to maintain a very tight time schedule.

My gratitude is to Professor Robert Morace of Daemen College Amherst, NY, USA with whom I struck a friendship during his visit to Kolkata a few months ago. He took off from his hectic teaching and research schedule to read my first two books on Sri Sri Ramakrishna, also published and marketed by Allied Publishers. I was very happy when he mailed me his comments on my published work on his return to his home base. I was still happier when he readily agreed to write a short Foreword to this book of mine as he found the treatment interesting when I discussed with him on mail. Thanks a lot Professor Morace!!

Finally, I thank the hundreds of readers who have read my earlier three books on Sri Sri Ramakrishna and shared their feedback. It was indeed a most pleasant surprise when I was informed that my book *The Real Ramakrishna: As I Have Come to Know Him as Ramakrishna's Child* (Noida: Allied Publishers, 2024) had been selected for the *Golden Book Award 2025*.

The Book: Its Purposes

If *Science*, which is generally grossly physical, reductionistic and materialistic, is at one bank of the river of knowledge, *Spirituality* is on the other, like Art. There is no bridge so that one can cross over. My one main purpose in this book is to build such a bridge as, according to *Isha Upanishad*, one must cultivate spiritual knowledge side by side with material and physical knowledge. That makes a *balanced mind*, ready for holistic understanding of any situation or subject.

My other purpose is to make a humble endeavour to show, through some examples, that the Hindu religion is the only one where some major and critical cosmic and astronomical phenomena have been most metaphorically and symbolically expressed through the concepts and conduct of the gods and goddesses and how they are linked with the behaviour of the Spiritual Super Souls like Bhagawan Sri Krishna Chaitanya and Sri Sri Ramakrishna.

God cannot be born. He is ageless and timeless. Still, according to the Hindu concepts, He uses his own super powers to take birth in different forms of gods and goddesses like the apparently ageless and timeless planets and stars that we are familiar with. His representative gods and goddesses also take birth as *avatars* (full or partial) who descend on earth to solve most critical problems which cannot be solved by ordinary members of the human kind.

To quote Sri Sri Ramakrishna: "When the *avatars* descend, millions and billions of people get their problems solved with their help and intervention......They can easily be compared to rail engines which carry hundreds of wagons or compartments loaded with passengers. *Avatars* cannot be easily understood or recognised by common people. They look just like them because of their *gross bodies* which are no different from other humans. They have hunger, thirst, illnesses and diseases just like normal people. Birth in the human form as an *avatar* also provides ample opportunity for 'sports' (*leela*) which is not possible in the godly form. However, if you want to know God or His *avatar* thoroughly, you must perform *sadhana* to build a bridge with Him."

Bhagawan Sri Krishna Himself says in Srimad Bhagabad Gita:

> "I am birthless, deathless and eternally present.
>
> Still, being the Supreme Lord of everything and all that you see, taking the help of 'Nature' – that is, using my own powers, I take birth and descend on earth." (4/6)

Let us take a look at the famous poem 'Fire and Ice' by the renowned American poet Robert Frost (1874–1963) who had earned the most prestigious Pulitzer Prize, not just once, but three times.

Fire and Ice

Some say the world will end in fire
Some say in ice
From what I've tasted of desire
I hold with those who favour fire
But if it had to perish twice,
I think I know enough of hate
To say that for destruction ice is also great
And would suffice.

(Published in *Harper's Magazine*, December 1920 and later in his 1923 Pulitzer Prize-winning book *New Hampshire*. It is one of Frost's best-known and most anthologized poems.)

The poet is talking about the *apocalypse*. In his perception, 'fire' stands for 'desire' whereas 'ice' represents 'hatred', both having a wide range each. 'Desire' could range from 'physical gratification' to the need for 'money, prestige, status, power, and authority'. And, 'hatred' can range from 'casteism, class bar, and colour prejudice' to 'political hatred' where love and compassion have become frozen like ice.

"In an anecdote, Frost recounted in 1960 in a 'Science and the Arts' presentation, the prominent astronomer Harlow Shapely claims to have inspired 'Fire and Ice'. Shapely describes an encounter he had with Frost a year before the poem was published in which Frost, knowing that Shapely was the astronomer of the day, asked him how the world will end. Shapely responded that either the sun will explode and incinerate the Earth, or the Earth will somehow escape this fate only to end up slowly freezing in deep space. Shapely was surprised at seeing 'Fire and Ice' in print a year later, and referred to it as how science can influence the creation of art, or clarify its meaning."

This is an experimental journey for me to see whether and how I can build a bridge between *astronomy & cosmic sciences* and *the art of spirituality.*

References

[1] "Isha Upanishad" – *Wikipedia.*

[2] "Dialogue between Sri Chaitanya Mahaprabhu and Ramananda Ray" – June 1989, Video Presentation on You Tube by Gopal Krishna Goswami.

[3] Suman Bhattacharya, *Dui Avatar: Sri Chaitanya O Sri Ramakrishna* (In Bengali), Kolkata: Girija Library, 2020, p. 12.

[4] "Fire and Ice (poem)" – *Wikipedia.*

[5] Deirdre J. Fagan, *Critical companion to Robert Frost: A Literary Reference to His Life and Work*, New York: Infobase Publishing, 2007, pp. 115–16.

[6] Tom Hansen, "Frost's 'Fire and Ice'", *The Explicator*, 2000, Vol. 59, No/Issue 4, pp. 27–30.

[7] Jeffrey Myers, *Robert Frost: A Biography*, New York: Replica Books (Penguin Random House), 2001.

Super Scientist Albert Einstein on Religion: Einstein's God Letter

In 1929, a *rabbi* from New York aware of Einstein's Jewish roots had sent him a telegram asking about his religious beliefs. Einstein replied that he did not believe in a God who controls the destinies of people, but in a God who manifests in the harmonious laws of existence. However, it seems that throughout his life and works, he understood that the world is far more complex than even the greatest minds can conceive.

In 2018, a letter from Albert Einstein known as the *GOD LETTER* was sold at auction for nearly 3 million US dollars. The letter was written in 1954 and addressed to a German philosopher Eric Gutkind who worked at the Princeton University. In that letter, he wrote that, though skeptical of religions, the scientists acknowledged the possibility of a grand spirit in nature – one that surpasses human nature and is beyond our comprehension. He believed that with the spiritual evolution of humanity, it is becoming increasingly clear that true religiosity is not based on the fear of death, nor blind faith but rather on striving for rational understanding. We all dance to the music of an invisible musician. The human life is subject to forces that we cannot control. Whether it be people, plants or cosmic dust, we all move to the melody played for us by an invisible musician beyond our perception. There is no room for chance in the world. Everything is governed by mathematical equations and formulae. Everything happens under the influence of forces beyond our control.

[Reference

[1] "63 Years Hidden! Einstein Reveals God and Religion", Video Presentation on You Tube, Memory Mosaic Channel.]

The Five-Faced Hindu God: Heramba

(A Form of Lord Ganesha)

I chose Lord Ganesha for three main reasons. Firstly, because, to my knowledge, He is the only mythological God who, having the head of an elephant, has a dark face; *darkness* is of interest to me in the present venture of mine. A white elephant (also an *albino*) is a rare kind of elephant, but not a distinct species.

Five Faced Hindu God

[As of 2023, Myanmar had ten white elephants and in 2016, the King of Thailand had eleven such animals. In Hindu *puranas*, the vehicle or mount of God Indra is the sacred white elephant named *Airavata* typically with four tusks in India and sometimes with five heads in Southeast Asia. King Bimbisar had a white bull elephant, which he had captured in a forest.

The white elephant also holds significance in the story of The Buddha's conception and birth. According to the story of the Buddha's conception, on the night Siddhartha was conceived, Queen Maya dreamt that a white elephant with six white tusks entered her right side. From this dream, soothsayers predicted that the child would be born a

Buddha or a Chakravarti (universal ruler). The white elephant is closely linked with Buddhist cosmology, because of the white elephant's close association with the planet *Sakra* – the chief *deva* of Mount Meru, and the concept of kingship.

In Western cultures, particularly in English, the term *white elephant* has come to mean a spectacular and prestigious thing that is more trouble than it is worth, or has outlived its usefulness to the person who owns it. While the item may be useful to others, its current owner would usually be glad to be rid of it.] (References 1 & 2)

Considering all aspects, I would prefer to have my Lord Ganesha with a dark head and face to avoid any confusion and controversy.

My second reason for choosing Lord Ganesha's *Heramba* or *Panchamukha* form is for its five heads and faces, representing the five *koshas*: the Annamaya Kosha (the visible body made of tissues, blood and other matter), the Pranamaya Kosha (the breath or life-force that provides energy and keeps the body active till death), the Monomaya Kosha (the emotional and relationship-related aspect), the Vijnanamaya Kosha (the intellectual aspect, representing upper consciousness) and the Anandamaya Kosha (the body of spiritual & cosmic bliss). The five great souls that I've chosen for my study and discussion – all had their gross bodies composed of all these five *koshas.* There is no other god or goddess in Hindu *puranas* who has been given this kind of a form (*rupa*, in Sanskrit). *Heramba* is the only one coming close to the human form. This form is important in *Tantric* worship of Ganesha and is popular in Nepal. (References 3–5)

The third reason for my choosing *Heramba*, a form of Lord Ganesha was because Ganesha was a product of *creation* (as you will see from what follows) and not of *procreation* which needs the involvement of both genders – masculine and feminine. *Creation* is an outcome of a single person – may be a male, or a female. *Creativity* comes from *'divya bhava'* (post-human/divine/spiritual moods) whereas *procreation* is possible in the *'poshu'* (pre-human) as well as *'naro'* (human) states of existence. (Reference 6)

As I chose *Heramba* as my adorable deity for my current project, I came across a beautiful little poem (as below) by an anonymous poet which made my eyes moist as I could really feel his vibrations in all my *koshas*:

Awakening

"I asked for His help
I called on His name
One of His many Names.

I asked not for myself
I sought help for many
And for what seemed insurmountable.

And as I prayed
I felt His presence wash over me
Calming me, soothing me, stilling me
Wrapping me in his warmth
Until all I could do was stop
And be still and feel His presence
And love Him."

Ganesha is Created

Lord Shiva was never a householder type. He was a wanderer. Where he would be was anybody's guess. His wife, Goddess Parvati used to live at Mount Kailash. One day, she was preparing for a bath. As she didn't want to be disturbed, she called Nandi, her husband Shiva's Bull and asked it to be at the door of her home as a guard and let no one pass or enter. Nandi faithfully took its post, intending to carry out Parvati's wishes. But, meanwhile, Lord Shiva appeared all of a sudden and wanted to enter into the house. Nandi had to allow him as, the beast being Lord Shiva's companion, its first allegiance was to the God.

Parvati was most upset at this gesture of Nandi. She was frustrated as she had no one as loyal as Nandi was to Shiva. She could not have any child also as her husband Shiva was not too keen to have any offspring as he practised celibacy. So, Parvati was determined to *create* a child herself.

She had already put some turmeric paste on her body before her bath. She took some paste from her body and breathed life into it. Immediately, her son was *created* to be most loyal to her and absolutely her own. She named him Ganesha.

After a few days, Parvati went for a bath, she posted Ganesha on guard duty at the door. Meanwhile, Shiva had disappeared but he suddenly appeared in front of their abode. This time, he found this strange boy telling him that he couldn't enter and Ganesha also did not know who this strange man was. Shiva got furious and he ordered his army to destroy the boy, but all the soldiers failed because Ganesha was supremely powerful having been *created* by Goddess Parvati.

This surprised Lord Shiva. Seeing that he was not an ordinary boy, the usually quiet, reserved and peace-loving Shiva decided he would have to fight and kill him. In his divine fury, Shiva severed Ganesha's head, killing him instantly. Witnessing this, Parvati was so enraged that she was determined to destroy the entire creation. Naturally, Brahma, the God of Creation intervened and requested Parvati to reconsider her plan. She said, she certainly would, but if only two conditions were met: one, that Ganesha be brought back to life; and, two, that he be forever worshipped before all other gods and goddesses.

Shiva, having cooled down by this time, and realising his mistake, agreed to Parvati's conditions. He sent Brahma out with orders to bring back the head of the very first creature he crossed that was laying with its head facing North. Brahma soon returned with the head of a strong and powerful elephant (dark or white is not mentioned anywhere in the puranic literature). Shiva quickly placed it on Ganesha's body.

Breathing new life into him, he declared Ganesha to be his own son and gave him the status of being foremost among the gods, and leader of all *ganas* (classes of beings). Ganesha thus became *Ganapati.*

Inner Meaning of the Story

Parvati is a goddess, the *Parashakti* (Supreme Energy). In the human body, she resides in the *muladhara chakra* as the *kundalini shakti.* 'Kundalini', thus, is the *divine energy* that we possess within ourselves.

My interpretation is like this. As long as a newborn infant cannot stand on its own legs, it feels diffident and not 'grounded'. The moment it can stand and walk a little without anybody's help, it becomes *conscious* of its own identity and its *ego* develops. The *ego* makes it feel 'grounded'. Its biological energy, from its whole body, flows into the ground, due to gravity. This makes the *kundalini shakti*, that had been acquired over millions of years by living in all the different types of creaturely forms, closeted in the lowermost *muladhar chakra* at the base of the spine. Lower extremity handicapped and bed-ridden people, who cannot stand on their legs or walk using their legs, their *egos* are shattered.

The *Sada Ripus* (the 'Six Enemies of the Mind') raise their heads only when we have an *ego* – the 'I' feeling, as we become conscious of our own identity, separate from others' and start 'comparing' and may end up in 'competition' instead of 'co-operation'. It is said that when we purify ourselves, ridding ourselves of the impurities (mainly the *Sada Ripus* – the *Six Enemies of the Mind*), only then the divine energy automatically comes within our reach.

Nandi, Shiva's bull, whom Parvati first assigned the responsibility to guard the door represents the divine temperament because of his 'unconditional devotion'. Nandi was so devoted to Shiva that his every thought was directed to Him. Nandi's such divine temperament had allowed it to win the trust of Parvati who assigned some major responsibility to it. Only such pure divine temperament, free from any *ripu*, qualifies one to gain access to the Devi's (the *kundalini shakti*'s) abode.

After Nandi permitted Shiva to enter, Parvati was disillusioned as she had never expected such a conduct from Nandi. On a sudden second thought she became aware of her own *creative* power. She thus took the turmeric paste, which she was using for her bath, from Her own body, and with it *created* Ganesha. Ganesha is the deity who guards the *muladhara chakra*, which is associated with the 'earth' element. In our body, the 'earth' element is represented by our bones and tissues which are our connections to the ground. Ganesha insists that we connect ourselves to our bodies and to the earth. For many people, there is disconnect from our bodies. We move through daily routine without conscious attention to our actions. We eat too quickly or distractedly, spend more time in our head than in our body; we only pay attention to our body when it gives us a signal.

Devi needed to *create* Ganesha, who represents the earthbound awareness, as a shield to protect the divine secret from unripe minds. It is when the awareness begins to turn away from things of the world, and towards the Divine, as Nandi had, that the great secret is revealed.

Shiva is the Lord and the Supreme Teacher. Ganesha here represents the ego-bound *Jiva*. When the Lord comes, the *Jiva*, surrounded as it is with the murky cloud of *ego*, usually doesn't recognise Him, and may even end up arguing or fighting with Him! Therefore, it is the duty of the Lord, in the form of the *Guru*, to cut off the head of our *ego*. So powerful is the *ego*, however, that at first the *Guru's* instruction may not work, as Shiva's armies failed to subdue Ganesha. It often requires a tougher approach, but, eventually the compassionate *Guru*, in His wisdom, finds a way.

Devi, threatened to destroy the whole 'Creation' after learning of Ganesha's demise. This indicates that when the *ego* thus dies, the liberated *Jiva* loses interest in the temporary physical vehicle, the body, and begins to merge with the *Supreme*. The physical world is here represented by Devi. This impermanent and changeable creation is a form of Devi to which this body belongs; the unchanging ABSOLUTE is Shiva, to which belongs the *Soul*. When the *ego* dies, the external world, which depends on the *ego* for its existence, disappears along with it. It is said that if we want to know the secrets of the world, which is manifestation of Devi, then we must first receive the blessings of Ganesha.

Shiva restoring life to Ganesha, and replacing its head with an elephant's means that before we can leave the body, the Lord first replaces our small 'selfish' *ego* with a big 'universal' *ego.* This doesn't mean we become more egoistic. On the contrary, we no longer identify with the limited individual self, but rather with the larger universal self. In this way, our life is renewed to become one that can truly benefit *Creation.* It is, however, only a functional *ego* like the one Krishna and Buddha kept. It is like a thin string tying the liberated 'consciousness' to our world, for our benefit.

Ganesha is given dominance over the *Ganas* which is a general term denoting all classes of beings, ranging from microbes, insects, amphibians, birds, animals and humans to the subtle and celestial beings. These various beings all contribute to the government of the Creation, everything from natural forces like storms and earthquakes to the elemental qualities like fire and water, to the functioning of the body's organs and processes. If we don't honour the *Ganas,* then our every action is a form of thievery as it is unsanctioned. Therefore, instead of propitiating each *Gana* in order to receive their blessings, we bow to their Lord, the Ganapati. By receiving His grace, we receive the grace of all. He removes any potential obstacles and enables our endeavours to succeed.

Heramba Ganapati

The *Mudgala Purana* mentions Heramba Ganapati as one of the thirty-two names of Ganesha. The *Skanda Purana* lists that Heramba Vinayaka as one of the fifty-six Vinayakas in the vicinity of Varanasi. The *Brahma Vaivarta Purana* explains the meaning of Heramba: the syllable *'he'* denotes helplessness or weakness, while *'ramba'* is protection of the weak, to save them from harm; thus Heramba means the 'Protection of the weak and good people'.

The colours of Heramba's heads closely relate to five aspects of his father Shiva – Ishana, Tatpurusha, Aghora, Vamadeva, and Sadyojata.

Heramba hides his *vahana,* a mighty lion. The lion, represents the deity's royalty and fierce nature. The lion is said to be inherited from his mother Parvati, who often rides it. Dinka, the usual *vahana* of Ganesha – is a rat or a mouse, which symbolizes the ability to overcome anything to get what he wants. Heramba is usually depicted with a lion as well as Dinka.

Heramba has ten arms. He holds a *pasha* (noose), *danta* (his broken tusk), *akhsmala* (rosary), *parashu* (battle-axe), a three-headed *mudgara* (mallet), and the sweet *modak*. His two other arms are held in *Varadamudra* (the boon-giving gesture) and *Abhayamudra* (a gesture denoting protection of the devotee). Other descriptions add a garland and a fruit to the attributes in his hand. He may be depicted in sculpture holding an *ankusha* (an elephant goad) in one of his hands.

In some parts of India, Ganesha is depicted as celibate, but in others he is said to be married to both *Buddhi* ('Intelligence') and *Siddhi* ('Success'). Yet, other traditions, give him a third wife, *Riddhi* ('Prosperity'). Sometimes, a consort may be depicted seated on his lap and one of Heramba's hands cuddles her. (References 7–10)

Two Tales About Lord Ganesha

As a boy, while playing, Ganesha found a cat who was after the life of his most loyal *vahana*, the mouse. He became furious and, in his rage, he started beating the cat which resulted in several cuts and bruises. The cat ran for his life.

When Ganesha calmed down and came to his mother Goddess Parvati, he was awe-struck to find her body full of cuts and bruises. It made him very upset and sad. When he asked how did she get those wounds on her body, in deep remorse she said that it was he who was responsible for those wounds. When Ganesha took her statement in utter surprise and asked how was it possible, she enquired whether he had beaten any creature the same morning. Ganesha told her about the cat who was after his loyal *vahana* the mouse. He admitted that he had beaten the cat a little while ago.

The Goddess told her he shouldn't have done so because she, as the source of Supreme female energy, is present in every female of every species while her husband Lord Shiva is present in every male member of every species. She said there was nothing in the universe except her female energy on every living female and her husband's male energy in every living male. Little Ganesha never had this knowledge and he was so regretful that he took a resolution to remain celibate (*brahmachari*) all his life as whoever he wanted to marry would have her mother's energy (and having a physical relationship with her will mean the Freudian *Oedipus Complex* – craving to have sex with one's own mother). His realisation, at a very young age, that the universe is nothing but a combination of male and female energy from both his parents was indeed a revelation for him that guided him throughout his life.

Now, the second tale. Once Goddess Parvati showed her gem-studded necklace to both her sons – Ganesha and Kartikeya and told them whoever amongst them would cover the fourteen worlds would get the necklace as a prize. Young Kartikeya thought, most smartly, he would easily win in this competition as he would ride on his *vahana*, the peacock and fly fast whereas his pot-bellied elder brother Ganesha whose *vahana* is the mouse would be lagging far behind. So, he started off. Ganesha took it easy – he was in a relaxing mood. He got up after a while to visualise the fourteen worlds being present in his parents' bodies – Hara-Parvati and went on chanting hymns in their praise. When Kartikeya returned, Parvati told him that Ganesha had already completed the task most cleverly to her total satisfaction and it was he who would be eligible to get the necklace. Kartikeya was fit and physically very active with his warrior-like temperament; but Ganesha, although fat and lazy, was the owner of a high degree of *practical intelligence*. This is the reason why every businessman and industrialist worships Lord Ganapati and he is worshipped first before offering puja to any God or Goddess. He is the symbol of wisdom – *siddhidata*. (References 11 & 12)

A Snippet Regarding Lord Ganesha

Amongst the different outfits of Lord Jagannath, one is the 'Elephant Dress'. When He puts it on, he adopts the form of the *Siddhi Data Ganesha*.

There is another opinion on this as well. Before the birth of Lord Buddha, His mother Maya Devi had dreamt of a white elephant entering into her womb. This is why on the day of *Snan Purnima*, Lord Jagannath is imagined as Lord Buddha and is dressed in the 'Elephant Dress'. On the wall of the Puri Jagannath temple, one can see Lord Jagannath's image in the place of Lord Buddha's as one of the ten *avatars* of Lord Vishnu. Before Sri Chaitanya introduced Lord Jagannath as Bhagawan Krishna, He used to be called 'Buddha-Jagannath'. (Reference 13)

References

[1] "Heramba" – *Wikipedia.*

[2] "White elephant (animal)" – *Wikipedia.*

[3] "*Kosha*" – *Wikipedia.*

[4] "Panchamukhi Ganesha: The Lord with Five Heads" – *Artisan's Crest*; *artisanscrest.com*

[5] "Panchamukha" – *Wikipedia.*

[6] "The Three Temperaments" – *Tantra Mag*, 6th January 2016.

[7] Amma, "Lord Ganesha: his birth story, symbolism, meaning and practice", *Online with Amma.*

[8] "Panchamukha" – *Wikipedia.*

[9] "Heramba" – *Wikipedia.*

[10] "Ganesh" – *Britannica.com*

[11] Swami Saradananda, *SriSri Ramakrishna Leela Prasanga* (In Bengali), Part 1, 'Sadhak Bhav', Kolkata: Udhbodhan Karjalaya, 1993, pp. 117–118.

[12] "Oedipus Complex" – *Wikipedia.*

[13] Tuhin Mukhopadhyay, *Chaitanyer Sesh Prahar*, (In Bengali), Kolkata: Patralekha, 7th Impression, 2023, pp. 73–74.

PART ONE

Three Super Souls – Material & Physical

Sir James Watt
(Engineering)

Sir Adam Smith
(Economics)

Sir William Thomson (Lord Kelvin)
(Natural Philosophy – Physics)

Sir James Watt

Sir Adam Smith

Lord Kelvin

CHAPTER 1

Three Super Souls

I sometimes forget that
I was created for joy
My mind is too busy
My heart is too heavy
Heavy for me to remember
that I have been
called to dance
the sacred dance for life
I was created to smile
to love
to be lifted up
O sacred one
Untangle my feet
from all that ensnares
Free my soul
That we might
dance
and that our dancing
might be contagious.

—Hafiz, ***Persian lyric poet***

"Go, wondrous creature! Mount where Science guides;
Go measure earth, weigh air, and state the tides;
Instruct the planets in what orbs to run,
Correct old Time, and regulate the sun;"

—Alexander Pope, ***An Essay on Man, 1733–1734***

A Revelation

The year was 1962, and the month was late September. The season was *fall* in the western world. I climbed the incline, along the University Avenue, to reach the Gilmorehill campus of the University of Glasgow (UoG), in Scotland, UK where I had been admitted for my post-graduate research studies. I had most unexpected goosebumps as I was putting my feet on the bottle-green grass of the fourth oldest English-speaking university of the world, established in 1451. Barring a few new buildings like the most modern Indoor Sports Complex, all the old structures had Neo-Gothic architecture typical of the 12th to 18th century in medieval Europe. Ranked 78 in QS World University Rankings 2025, it is one of Scotland's four ancient universities, the other three being St. Andrews (Scotland's first university, which was attended by King Charles's two sons Prince William & Prince Harry), Aberdeen & Edinburgh.

During the period 1940 to 2000, Glasgow was the Mecca of Engineering and Edinburgh, the Mecca of Medicine. All highly aspiring engineering and medical students from all countries of the world used to flock to these two universities. The UoG campus was most picturesque, located on top of a hillock, with the rivulet Kelvin meandering through it towards its meeting point with a larger River Clyde. As I was appreciating the beauty of the campus with its greeneries and the dark grey Gothic buildings, I came face to face with something which was unthinkable in the country, where I came from.

There were two campus cleaners with their hands engaged in broomsticks. Both were whistling a Scottish Highland tune and sweeping away with great fun and enjoyment. Quite an unseen scene in India. The campus cleaners of Jadavpur University wherefrom I graduated would do their work most grudgingly as, in our country, the sweepers belong to the untouchable class – a distance is maintained from them by the students, faculty, and university staff. I pulled up myself, mustered courage and began to talk to these two blokes. I enquired: "Excuse me please! You seem to enjoy your work immensely, cleaning up the campus. I have never seen it happening in India, the country I come from. What is it that makes you so happy and proud about your work? May I know please?"

"Oh, My, my!!" The answer came promptly from one of them. "We have one of the most important assignments, that one can think of. And that is of keeping the campus of the 4th oldest English- speaking university in the world clean and tidy. Shouldn't that make us motivated and proud?"

The other man now joined in: "Do you know that the University has the footprints of three most memorable pioneers, whose names and deeds will never be erased from the pages of history? If you've a few minutes, we will take you round to meet them in the form of basalt stone." It was an invitation I readily accepted.

First, we went to the statue of Sir James Watt, the engineering genius and inventor of the steam engine, whose name I was familiar with being a student of engineering. Besides, the Engineering Building where I was going to have my research lab, had a huge, well spread-out Sir James Watt Engineering Laboratory.

The two janitors (as the campus cleaners are designated in the English-speaking world) now took me to the statue of Sir Adam Smith. Smith, who was the father of 'Economics' was the Professor of Moral Philosophy at UoG for his whole life. His name was also familiar as I had heard it from Prof. Amartya Sen (later Economics Nobel Laureate in 1998) who used to teach us Economics during the first two years of our engineering programme. Dr Triguna Sen, the Jadavpur University Vice Chancellor, had his higher education in Germany where engineering students had to study Economics for two solid years. So, he had brought young Amartya fresh from Cambridge. And, in his very first class with us, Sen had asked us: "How many of you know who was the Father of Economics?" As none of us could answer, he answered it for us.

The third life-size statue where we stopped was that of William Thomson (later Lord Kelvin), who was Professor of Natural Philosophy at the UoG for 53 years. He loved The University so much that he never left to join the faculty elsewhere despite fabulous offers.

Sir James Watt and Sir Adam Smith

Regarding these two great souls, although I do not have much to say, even whatever little I tell you, it will be something new for you.

When I went for admission in the College of Engineering & Technology (CET), Jadavpur University, Calcutta in 1957, I had to face an interview board. Dr Triguna Sen, the then Vice-Chancellor was in chair. Later, he became the Minister of Education, Govt. of India and shifted to New Delhi.

Dr Sen looked at my application form and the attached documents and said straight away: "Young man, you've very good marks. Naturally, I presume, you want to join the Mechanical Engineering degree course." I answered straight on his face, although most humbly: "Sir, how many mechanical engineers design a new machine? They are all mostly engaged in the repair and maintenance of machines which are already installed. Isn't it?"

Dr Sen looked straight into my eyes and said: "Oh! My boy! You seem to be different." He looked at the other members of the interview board and said: "Look! Here is Mr Different! He wants to be like Sir James Watt of Glasgow who had invented the steam engine."

Then, he went on to say: "Then he will not be interested in Electrical, Chemical and Telecommunication. Let us put him into Civil Engineering with major in Architecture in the Final Year, so that he gets the opportunity for designing buildings, bridges, dams and airports."

That idea appealed to me and I opted for Civil Engineering. Later on, at the UoG, I again came across Sir James Watt and, this time, very close to him as I had to work in the Sir James Watt Engineering Laboratory. Much later, when I specialised in *Bioengineering*, since I was concentrating on humans only, I developed *Human Engineering* to encompass the studies on the human body, brain, mind and soul from an engineering point of view. I also wrote a book by the title of *Human Engineering for Better Management.* My association with Sir James Watt got reinforced when I studied in somewhat depth the poems and songs of the Bengali minstrel Fakir Lalon Shah, the Baul maestro, who had conceived the human body as a masterpiece of engineering and pioneered the domain of *Deha Tattva,* dealing with the engineering aspects of the human body.

I have already told you that I came to know about Sir Adam Smith from Prof. Amartya Sen who used to teach us Economics in the 1st and 2nd Years of the engineering course. I had to study Economics again – both 'Business Economics' and 'Industrial Economics' while attending the 'Management' programme at the British Institute of Management, London. But, the most interesting encounter that I had with Economics when I was studying *Brain Science.*

Professor Paul Zak was an economist in USA. While doing some research on industrial economics, he came across two business organisations having the same product range, competing with each other but one was doing much better than the other. He was indeed intrigued and discussed the matter with his wife who had happened to be a medical doctor, specialising in neurology. She suggested him to take a course in *neuroscience.* He made a thorough study of the human brain and its functions and had a hunch that possibly in the organisation which was doing much better than the other, there was a much better teamwork. Effective teamwork means the team members are most understanding and co-operative; that they are very well-bonded with each other. He located the brain chemical which is responsible for this mutual bonding and trust. It was *Oxytocin* (*'O'*) which is secreted from the brain's 'Pituitary Glands' ('PiG'). He took blood samples to find out the level of *'O'* in the blood of the team members of both organisations. Amazingly, it was found that all the team members of the 'winning' organisation had a high *'O'* level whereas in the case of the members of the 'losing' organisation, it was low. He got the fillip to do a massive study and founded the hybrid science of *Neuro-Economics (NE).*

So, being a scholar of *Brain Sciences,* I have to come across *NE* regularly in course of my scholarly studies and research. So, Sir Adam Smith's soul is very much with me in my present domain of work. (References 1–5)

Lord Kelvin

During the reign of Queen Victoria, Glasgow became the 'second city' and workshop of the British Empire. Over the same period, William Thomson (1824-1907) rose from a college student to the first Lord of British science, Lord Kelvin, Baron of Largs. On his death, he was given a resting place alongside Sir Isaac Newton in Westminster Abbey.

Lord Kelvin was born William Thomson in Belfast, Ireland. As professor of Nat Phil (as 'Science' was known in the ancient British universities – short form for 'Natural Philosophy'), he was instrumental in the formulation of the first and second laws of THEROMODYNAMICS, and contributed significantly to unifying PHYSICS, which was then in its infancy of development as an emerging academic discipline.

He was the President of the Royal Society from 1890 to 1895 and was the first scientist to be elevated to the British House of Lords, and came to be known as the 1st Baron Kelvin. The 'Kelvin' name was adopted from the River Kelvin that flows through the UoG campus which was very dear to his heart. It was not unlikely that he had most of his brainwaves related to physical phenomena – both 'gross' and 'subtle' while taking walks along the rivulet or while smoking his pipe sitting on a cast iron bench on the riverbank.

Lord Kelvin's Interest in 'Dark Matter'

Lord Kelvin firmly believed that *Science Is Measurement* and whatever he bumped on to, he tried to 'measure'. He didn't spare to measure the celestial bodies also.

Lord Kelvin's interest in the DARK MATTER is relatively unknown. In a talk given in the USA in1884, Lord Kelvin estimated the number of dark bodies in the *Milky Way* from the observed velocity dispersion of the stars orbiting around the centre of the galaxy. By using these measurements, he estimated the mass of the galaxy, which he determined from the mass of the visible stars.

Lord Kelvin thus concluded that many of our stars, perhaps a great majority of them, may be DARK BODIES. Henri Poincare

(1854–1912), the French mathematician, in 'The Milky Way and Theory of Gases' used the French term *maitere obscure* ("dark matter") in discussing Kelvin's work. (References 6 & 7)

Lord Kelvin's Early Life

The early life of a scientist is most important to explore when and how the seed for future excellence was sown. Kelvin attended Glasgow University classes from the age 10, as his father left Ireland to become the Professor of Mathematics at the UoG. He wrote his first scientific paper, under the pseudonym 'PQR', aged only 16. In his teens, he learned French to read the work of the famous French mathematician Fourier, famous for his brainchild – the 'Fourier Series'.

Fourth of 7 children, his father James brought him up as his mother died early. The family relocated to Scotland in the early 1830s, where Kelvin's father James accepted the mathematics chair at the UoG, as I've already mentioned. The 16-year-old boy by the name of William Thomson, spent his summer vacation studying an extraordinarily sophisticated mathematical controversy. His brilliant analysis inspired lavish praise and made the boy an instant intellectual celebrity.

Lord Kelvin's Work on Astronomy

Lord Kelvin's, (for whom the Kelvin absolute temperature scale is named), scientific achievements ranged across the study of ENERGY and HEAT. He had very strong views on the age of the Sun and the Earth based on his understanding of thermo-dynamics. He viewed the Sun as the incubator that kept all life on Earth alive. Although, later on, other scientists established that the Sun is powered by the fusion of hydrogen nuclei, Kelvin's bold attempt to make scientific judgements was indeed most exemplary at that era of infancy of modern reductionist science.

In school, William Thomson (later Lord Kelvin who became the Chancellor of the University of Glasgow), showed a keen interest in the *classics* along with his interest in the *sciences*. At age 12, he won a prize for translating Lucian of Samosata's *Dialogues of the Gods* from ancient

Greek into English. In the academic year 1839/1840, Thomson won the class prize in *astronomy* for his "Essay on the figure of the earth" which showed an early facility for mathematical analysis and creativity.

References

[1] "University of Glasgow" – *Wikipedia.*

[2] "Sir James Watt" – *Wikipedia.*

[3] "Sir Adam Smith" – *Wikipedia.*

[4] "Lord Kelvin" – *Wikipedia.*

[5] Paul J. Zak, *The Moral Molecule: How Trust Works,* New York: Plume (The Penguin Group), 2013.

[6] C. Smith, "Lord Kelvin: scientist of energy", *IOP SCIENCE, Superconductor Science and Technology,* 1991, Vol. 4, No. 9, p. 502.

[7] Pankaj Kherka, 'Dark Matter and Dark Energy' – Dissertation submitted at the SRM University, Gangtok, Sikkim, India in 2022.

CHAPTER 2

Dark Matter & Dark Energy

"Is the whole of life visible to us, or do we in fact know only the one hemisphere before we die?"

—***Vincent van Gogh*** *(1853–1890),*
Dutch painter

"So strong was that imprint [of the night sky] that I'm certain that I had no choice in the matter, that in fact, the universe called me".

— ***Dr Neil de Grasse Tyson*** *(1958–),*
American astrophysicist and author of
Death By Black Hole and Other Cosmic Quandaries,
New York: WW Norton, 2007.

Lord Kelvin and Sri Sri Ramakrishna

Lord Kelvin conducted a Master Class at Johns Hopkins University, Baltimore, USA on the new dimensions of natural philosophy. Starting from his lecture series in 1884, he was the very first scientist in the world to formulate the hypothetical concept of *DARK MATTER* which does not interact with light or other electromagnetic radiation. He also attempted to define and locate some 'dark bodies' in the *Milky Way.*

Around the same time, Avatar Sri Sri Ramakrishna (1836-1886) was deeply immersed in the *DARK MATTER* of the dark Goddess Kali deriving his spiritual drive, from Kali's *DARK ENERGY.* Dark energy provided him with the accelerating spiritual force. The venue was the Dakshineswar Kali temple of the Bengal Province near Calcutta, the capital city of the then British India. Ramakrishna was not just a simple priest; he had already elevated himself to the position of the *spiritual child* of the dark Goddess.

Dark Matter

The term *dark matter* was coined by Fritz Zwicky (1898–1974) in 1933 at USA's California Institute of Technology to describe the unseen, invisible matter (that is why it is called *dark* matter) needed to explain the galaxies in the Coma Supercluster that contains over 1,000 identified galaxies. Zwicky showed that the galaxies of the Coma Cluster were moving too fast for the cluster to be bound together by the visible matter of its galaxies. He concluded that the galaxies must be held together by the invisible *dark matter.*

In the 1970s, Vera Rubin of the Carnegie Institute of Technology, USA, found evidence of *dark matter* in her research on galaxy rotation. *Dark matter* makes up most of the mass of galaxies and galaxy clusters. The qualities and behaviour of *dark matter*, the invisible 'glue' of the universe, continue to be shrouded in mystery.

While computer simulations suggest *dark matter* should pile up in a galaxy's centre, called a 'density cusp', many previous telescopic observations have indicated that it is instead more easily dispersed throughout a galaxy. The reason for this tension between the 'simulated model' and 'practical observation' continues to puzzle astronomers, reinforcing the mystery of the *dark matter.*

In astronomy, *DARK MATTER* is a hypothetical form of matter which is very choosy in its behaviour. It does not interact with light or other electromagnetic radiation. Dark matter is implied by gravitational effects that occur in the context of formation and evolution of galaxies and other cosmic phenomena.

In a cosmological model, the present-day observable universe contains only 5% ordinary or normal matter, 26.8% dark matter, and 68.2% dark energy. The other components such as *neutrinos* and *photons* are negligible. Thus, *dark matter* and *dark energy* constitute 95% of the total mass-energy content. *Dark matter* is classified as 'cold', 'warm' or 'hot' according to velocity. Recent models have favoured a 'cold dark matter' scenario. Scientific evidence points to dark matter being a new type of fundamental particle or particles that interact with 'normal' or 'ordinary' matter only through gravity.

The invisible mass does not emit light, nor does it reflect light; it is completely dark to our telescopes despite our most modern and advanced technology. All that we can see as the planets, stars, and galaxies comprise only 5 percent of the universe, 95 percent is pitch dark, unfathomable.

[Note: Sri Sri Ramakrishna's Goddess Kali, made of basalt stone was *cold dark matter*. It was the *Avatar* himself who provided it with the 'warmth' of love and compassion after life was infused into it by a *siddha* priest.]

Presence of *dark energy* was recognised by the 2011 Nobel Prize in Physics awarded to Saul Perlmutter of the Lawrence Berkeley National Laboratory and the University of California, Berkeley, Brian Schmidt of the Australian National University and Adam Riess of Johns Hopkins University and Space Telescope Science Institute, both in Baltimore, Maryland. However, cosmologists understand nothing about *dark energy* even though it appears to comprise about 68 to 70 percent of the universe that we know. They are desperately seeking to uncover its two most fundamental properties: its strength, and its permanence.

Cosmologists understand nothing about *dark energy* even though it comprises nearly 68 to 70 percent of the entire universe that is known to us.

Dark energy's density is very low, much less than the density of ordinary matter or *dark matter*, within galaxies. Is it thus possible, that the subtle-bodied souls who are floating in the space between its various levels, constitute the *dark energy* whereas the *dark matter* consists of the souls which are permanent residents of the post-death realm, including Dr Brian Weiss's *masters* and the gods, goddesses, avatars, prophets and all kinds of godmen whom I would describe as the *'great souls'*?

According to the *Nasadiya Sukta* of the *Rig Veda*, before the *Big Bang*, there was no time and no space. There was no *duality* – neither death, nor immortality; nor was there any night or day. Everything was *dark*. The cosmos now undergoes an infinite number of deaths and rebirths. Does it, by any chance, correspond to the deaths and rebirths of the subtle bodies or souls that come from the Earth after leaving the living bodies, post-death?

These are just two of the basic questions I have which need to be answered to develop a clear perception of what all happen in the space above us. (References 1–7)

From Kelvin's 'Dark Energy' to Higgs & Bose's 'God Particle'

In 1964, Peter Higgs theorised the existence of the Higgs Boson, which is a fundamental force-carrying particle associated with the Higgs field. The 'Higgs field' is a quantum field that gives mass to particles and exists throughout the universe. Higgs was responsible for one of the greatest discoveries in the twentieth century. His ground-breaking work helped explain how everything in the universe attains mass. In the 'Higgs field', the Higgs Boson acts as a wave and helps give mass to other fundamental particles through its interaction in terms of its vibration (oscillation). Researchers at the Large Hadron Collider, the most powerful particle accelerator in the world, discovered the particle much later – in 2012. Higgs was awarded the Nobel prize a year later.

Particles make up everything in the universe but they did not have any mass when the universe began. They all sped around at the speed of light. Everything we see – planets, stars and life – emerged after particles gained their mass from a fundamental field associated with the particle known as Higgs Boson.

In the media, the Higgs Boson has often been called the *god particle* after the 1993 book by Nobel Laureate physicist Leon Lederman which he titled the "Goddamn particle" – owing to the frustration over how difficult it was to detect. However, his publishers changed the name to 'The God Particle', which often draws ire from religious communities.

[Interestingly, Peter Higgs (1929–2024) was a professor at the University of Edinburgh in Scotland since the 1950s, just 84.4 km away from Lord Kelvin's Glasgow. Both the Scottish physicists, Kelvin and Higgs had taken up the challenge to unveil the mystery of the cosmos – the cosmic egg *Brahmanda*, which is the storehouse of eternal energy, the *Brahma*. More interestingly, the sub-atomic particles known as *Bosons* are named after the Indian physicist Satyendra Nath Bose from Calcutta, just 11.8 km away from Dakshineswar where Avatar Ramakrishna performed his sport (*leela*) with the Dark Goddess Kali.]

While Lord Kelvin was a practising Christian, Higgs was a life-long atheist and he disliked the name 'God particle'. Bose was a devout Hindu and an ardent nationalist. The Department of Science & Technology, Govt. of India, in one of its publications, has described Bose as the *'Forgotten Father of God Particle'*.

The accepted view today is that the universe started with a gigantic explosion called the 'Big Bang'. For fractions of a second after the 'Big Bang', the universe consisted of the most elementary constituents of matter interacting with each other through other particles which are carriers of different kinds of forces existing in Nature. And, the carriers of all forces in Nature are 'Bosons' or the *God particle* 'Higgs-Boson'. (References 8–10)

A Theory of the Universe (Purely speculative)

Science has revealed that electric charge gets developed in vacuum due to *stagnant effect.*

In this universe also there was vacuum. There was nothing anywhere. In course of time, 'Tremendous Electric Charge' got developed all over the universe due to *stagnant effect.* This unlimited electric charge got collided in neutral zone creating tremendous heat, echoed gigantic sound 'OM' and produced byproducts. [Today's scientific world calls it Big Bang]. It resulted in generating two universes ....

1. A *Visible* universe ... which comprises solid, liquid, gas, rays, and everything else that is visible to human eye or can be detected by scientific instruments.
2. An *Invisible* universe, that appears *dark* to us as light cannot pass through it. It consists of *souls.* [Spiritual or Cosmic energy, which is *dark*]. There is infinite number of souls in this universe. Soul is the fundamental force of universe and is immortal. Strength of souls varies widely. Souls are free as well as entrapped. Space

occupied by invisible universe is far more than visible universe, as it is the *dark matter* and *dark energy* combined.

Soul is energy entrapped in material. All planets, stars have entrapped soul power. That is why all planets follow the trajectory and keep moving. Even an atom has protons and neutrons bound together by soul power.

Magnet has flux around it. Similarly, soul has flux around it, which is known as the *aura.* Soul + *aura* decide the quality and power of soul. The quality and power of souls vary widely.

Supreme souls – gods and demons – have supreme *aura*: well spread-out, while ordinary souls – human and other species on earth – have ordinary *aura.*

Soul + *aura* – decides the quality and power of the soul. It has affinity to build suitable home [physique/morphic form] to reside by using *pancha bhuta*: earth, water, fire, air and ether. The nature of morphology of each species varies widely. Thus, various species including the human got created on earth or other parts of the universe independently under suitable tropical conditions.

The supreme or superior souls are created outside the solar system. They did land on earth to establish their rule. They were termed as gods and demons. The relics of some ancient structures on earth and scriptures are the evidences about their existence on earth in the ancient past. They used to engage in conflicts and wars too. The *aura* was used as a weapon, a *spiritual weapon.* The last God physically active on earth was Lord Krishna. He killed all devils on earth. He also guided on the philosophy of life for a common man vide GEETA – which was narrated to the warrior Arjun on the battlefield of Kurukshetra. The philosophy of life included the paths to follow – *Karma Yoga, Jnana Yoga, Dhyana Yoga,* and *Bhakti Yoga.*

The first humans – both male and female – were thus got created in Africa before they spread out to the other parts of the world, as far as paleontological research has revealed. They later produced their kind as reproductive organs were inbuilt naturally. That is why the appearance of human in different parts of earth differs. There was hybrid production also later. (Reference 11)

Universal Energy Budget

The 'Universal Energy Budget' can be represented by a *pie chart*, where only 5 percent of the universe is 'normal matter' (or 'ordinary matter') which consists of everything visible. It is what we see and interact with every moment. In the balance 95 percent, 27 percent is the *dark matter* and 68 percent is *dark energy. Dark matter* means the matter that we can't see, because it does not interact with light like the 'normal matter' does. It does not emit, absorb or reflect light in the normal way. It interacts very weakly or almost not at all with 'normal matter' that we and our measuring instruments are made of. Thus, *dark matter* cannot be measured by normal means. The exception is that *dark matter* does exert gravitational attraction, just like 'normal matter'. Sir Isaac Newton demonstrated in 1687 that matter attracts all other matter in the universe with the *force of gravity.*

Astronomers have studied *gravitational forces* in the universe at all distance scales (from the rotation of stars in galaxies, to the motion of galaxies in clusters, to the structure of the *cosmos* since the *BIG BANG*) for nearly a century. Surprisingly, the measured *gravity* far exceeds (by about five times) what can be explained by the 'normal' (or 'ordinary') matter. Basically, there's not enough 'normal matter' in the universe to explain why galaxies stay together or how they are formed in the first place.

Dark energy does not interact through any fundamental forces other than *gravity*. Its density is very low, much less than the density of the 'normal' or 'ordinary' matter within galaxies. It is dilute, believed to uniformly fill otherwise void empty space. *Dark energy* is an intrinsic, fundamental energy of space.

I have a few questions:

> Where do the *souls* of dead creatures go after leaving the dead bodies? *Souls* are *subtle bodies*. So, do they constitute the 'low-density' *dark energy* that fills the otherwise void empty space? Is it true that all the souls travelling to the space from the dead bodies on earth are being added to the *dark energy* mass in the space so the universe is expanding at an accelerating rate? Is it true that the 'Post-death

Realm' is *dark energy* which we cannot see? These are questions to be answered through inter-disciplinary research. (References 12 & 13)

Black Holes

It was a boat, a steamship, to be exact, out in the middle of the Atlantic Ocean. And, someone on board was scribbling out equations. It was not some white-skinned and white-haired Einstein, but a young dark brown-skinned, dark-haired kid, just 19 years old from India, Subrahmanyan Chandrasekhar. The young scholar was on the way to join the University of Cambridge in England on a scholarship for his post-graduate studies.

Chandra was born in 1910 when India was under the British rule. His uncle was the renowned physicist, C V Raman, who would later go on to be the first Indian to ever secure a Nobel Prize.

Chandra had made up his mind, pretty early, that he wanted to do science and he intended to prove himself. At 18, he was awarded a full scholarship to study at Cambridge. While on the boat to England, he realised that you have to combine quantum mechanics and relativity to calculate what happens to a star at the end of its life. He was the first to conceive the existence of *black holes*. In 1983, Chandrasekhar was awarded the Nobel Prize in physics for his discovery of the *black holes*.

Chandrasekhar was equally interested in literature and classical music. He used to play the *Veena.*

Black holes, which are present in the *cosmos*, are like wells. Nothing escapes from a *black hole*'s gravitational pull, which is so strong that even light cannot escape from being sucked into it.

In the context of 'Spiritual Super Souls' (3-S), my interpretation of *black holes* is that a 'Spiritual Super Soul' ('3-S') has the power to suck all the negativity, sins and misdeeds of a person having a negative nature and personality. (You will see, in later chapters, how Mahaprabhu Sri Krishna Chaitanya and Sri Sri Ramakrishna exercised their 'black hole' powers to transform negatively inclined persons).

White Holes

While a *black hole* sucks, swallows and consumes things irretrievably, a *white hole* expels or spits them out. It is a *black hole* running backwards in time. White holes cannot exist, since they violate the *Second Law of Thermodynamics.* They are thus purely hypothetical objects, but astronomers are contemplating how they could form in reality. (References 14–19)

Black Holes and Dark Energy

Black holes are of different types. I propose to classify them according to their size: normal black holes, larger than normal black holes, supernormal black holes, and supermassive black holes.

There is a claim by cosmologists that the mysterious *dark energy* that is accelerating the expansion of the universe could arise from supermassive *black holes* at the heart of galaxies.

According to general relativity, a *black hole* is a pure gravitational field so strong that its own energy sustains its existence. They are thought to emerge when massive stars collapse to an infinitesimal point, leaving just gravitational fields behind. Supermassive *black holes* having millions or billions of times the mass of our Sun are believed to lurk in the hearts of galaxies.

In 1966, Soviet physicist Erast Gliner showed Einstein's equation could also produce objects that, to outside observers, look and behave exactly like a *black hole* – yet are, in fact, giant balls of *vacuum energy.* If such objects were to exist, it would mean that rather than being uniformly spread throughout space, *dark energy* is actually confined to specific locations: the interior of *black holes.*

[*Note:* What is *vacuum energy* in the case of a totally 'devoted' devotee who has surrendered her/himself wholly to the God or Goddess she/he worships. Her/his soul would have no other thoughts – it will remain *vacuum* in a way, ready to 'suck' in the soul of any person who has a high spiritual potential.]

Astrophysicist Duncan Farrah of the University of Hawaii, Manoa and his colleagues studied elliptical galaxies and found that *black holes* in the early universe were much smaller relative to their host galaxy than those in the modern universe, indicating they had grown by a factor of 7 to 10 times in mass. This made them conclude that black holes were made of *dark energy*.

Now, *dark energy* rules the cosmos as it accounts for nearly 70 percent of the cosmic matter/energy budget. This wasn't always the case. Earlier, matter and gravity had ruled the universe. But, no one knows where the *dark energy* came from or how that switch from matter to *dark energy* happened.

Where in the modern-day universe is gravity as strong as it was at the beginning of the universe? The answer is only at the heart of the *black holes*. The investigating research team determined that *black holes* could be 'cosmically coupled' to *dark energy* whose density is not constant. (References 20–24)

Black Hole's *Dopamine* Hunger

Is a *black hole* Dopamine hungry? Yes, it is. Let us examine the behaviour of the dark Goddess Kali.

At the very beginning of his spiritual journey, Sri Sri Ramakrishna had realised, from the very deep core of his soul, that the All-powerful Goddess Kali is the highest entity for deriving pleasure from consumption, which satisfied her need for the 'feel good' neurochemical *Dopamine* (*'D'*). Her ways of earning *'D'* was most peculiar. She would suck and take away everything without any discrimination just like the *black holes* present in the universe. She would even consume 'time' and thus she was called *Kali*. At the end of her phase of such consumption would come *creation*. It is just like the female vagina which sucks the semen of the male and after effective fusion between the sperm and the ovum, a new *creation* comes into being. As a part of that great goddess, at every moment of our worldly existence, we look for pleasure from consumption.

Goddess Kali's ways of deriving pleasure are most weird. She slays the demons and earns her *'D'*, drinks their fresh blood, covers her private parts with the severed hands of those slain monsters to earn more *'D'*. She adorns her chest with a garland made from their severed heads. She makes the demons give up and accept defeat and dances the *tandava* like her husband Lord Shiva, holding a severed demon head in one of her hands. This is how she earns her *'D'*. All her *rajasic* actions are *tamasic* by nature but the ultimate aim is to fill the air with *sattvic* vibrations, as all the 'evils' have been eliminated.

Her conduct and all her acts for a noble cause did impress and influence Ramakrishna who, most contrarily, having left every object and opportunity for pleasure aside, had chosen the Goddess herself to earn his *Dopamine* and *Oxytocin* – respectively the 'smart' and 'sustained' happiness chemicals.

'Near Black Hole Experience' ('NBHE')

I am sharing with you one *kirtan* by Krishna Das which, if you blindly follow his style of singing, will give you a 'NBHE'.

American-born Jeffrey Kagel was fed up with the highly materialistic and a-spiritual American life and was inspired by Ram Dass (formerly Richard Alpert, 1931- 2019, a psychologist who was on the faculty of Harvard University) to visit Neem Karoli Baba's *ashram* in North India. Ram Dass believed in non-dualism – that there existed an unchanging and absolute entity – the Hindu *Brahman*, which he more frequently called God, the divine, the oneness, from which all material reality came. Kagel travelled to India in August 1970 and became the principal devotee of Neem Karoli Baba (Maharaj-Ji). His name Krishna Das was given by his guru who, after he had spent quite some time with him, instructed him to go back home and share with people whatever little spiritual knowledge he had acquired in India. Alpert had a beautiful voice and, since he could sing very well, he started reaching people in his homeland, in large gatherings, through his *kirtans*.

He was referred to as the 'Rockstar of Yoga' by the Grammys, when he was nominated for a 2013 Grammy Award for his 'Live Ananda' album.

I can assure you of getting spiritual vibes if you listen through his 'Om Namah Shivaya' live performance (available on You Tube) at the Church of St Paul and St Andrews, New York City on October 26, 2013.

The *kirtan* goes as follows:

"Om Namah Shivaya, Om Namah Shivaya, Om Namah Shivaya!
Om Namah Shivaya, Om Namah Shivaya, Om Namah Shivaya!
Shivaya Namah, Shivaya Namah, Om Namah Shivaya,

Shambhu Shankara, Namah Shivaya,
Girija Shankara, Namah Shivaya (x 4)
Arunachala Shiva, Namah Shivaya

Om Namah Shivaya, Om Namah Shivaya
Om Namah Shivaya, Om Namah Shivaya
Shambhu Shankara, Namah Shivaya
Shambhu Shankara, Namah Shivaya
Girija Shankara, Namah Shivaya
Girija Shankara, Namah Shivaya

Om Namah Shivaya, Namah Shivaya
Om Namah Shivaya, Namah Shivaya
Shambhu Shankara, Namah Shivaya
Girija Shankara, Namah Shivaya

Om Namah Shivaya, Om Namah Shivaya
Om Namah Shivaya, Om Namah Shivaya
Shambhu Shankara, Namah Shivaya
Girija Shankara, Namah Shivaya

Om Namah Shivaya, Om Namah Shivaya
Om Namah Shivaya, Om Namah Shivaya
Om Namah Shivaya, Namah Shivaya, Namah Shivaya
Om Namah Shivaya, Namah Shivaya, Namah Shivaya

Sambhu Shankara, Namah Shivaya
Girija Shankara, Namah Shivaya

Sambhu Shankara, Namah Shivaya
Girija Shankara, Namah Shivaya.

Om Namah Shivaya, Namah Shivaya, Namah Shivaya
Om Namah Shivaya, Namah Shivaya!!

The lead singer goes on repeating the stanzas in that order increasing the speed slowly and steadily as if the sonic vibrations are sucking the listener into the *kirtan* like the *black hole* sucks whatever comes in front of it. The listeners get immersed into the spiritual mood so intensely that the *Bliss Molecule 'Anandamide'* (*'ANA'/'AEA'*) gets secreted inside their brains giving an euphoric experience as one gets by smoking *cannabis.* It exerts an overall modulatory effect on the brain reward circuitry.

Cannabis is a 'phyto-cannabinoid' that is an external source of blissful experience. A team at the Hebrew University of Jerusalem, Israel was engaged in research on *cannabis* leaves and, in the process, they discovered that our brain and body have 'cannabinoid receptors'. Further pursuing their research endeavour Professor Raphael Mechoulam (1930–2023) and his team did identify 'endocannabinoids' in human biology. He is known as the 'godfather of cannabis research'. The cannabis plant produces *hashish* and *marijuana.* Mechoulam, initiated a research project that led to the isolation of the first described endocannabinoid *Anandamide* (AEA/ANA) in 1992. His post-doctoral researcher Lumir Ondrej Hanus borrowed the prefix *Ananda* (*'Bliss'*) from Sanskrit vocabulary and called it *Anandamide.*

The endocannabinoid system is a relatively newly discovered neurotransmitter system, which influences a variety of functions and systems in the human body. Once *Anandamide* (*ANA/AEA*) is made it travels to different parts of the body to have a de-stressing and relaxation effect. *ANA/AEA* also affects our mood and feelings. It helps us to learn better and feel less pain.

Now I share an American pop song, written by Cole Porter in 1936 and sung by Frank Sinatra once and then by Lady Gaga and Tony Bennett separately which indirectly means a 'black hole' experience in *love.*

"I've got you under my skin
I've got you deep in the heart of me
So deep in my heart that you're really a part of me
I've got you under my skin.
I tried so not to give in
I said to myself, 'this affair never shall go so well'
But why should I try to resist when, baby, I know so well
I've got you under my skin.

I'd sacrifice anything, come what might
For the sake of having you near
In spite of a warning voice that comes in the night
And repeats, repeats in my ear."

Dark Matter and Dark Energy in Hinduism

Hinduism, in general, believes in divine beings having forms. So, Hindus worship gods and goddesses in the form of idols. Any idol made of clay, stone, or metal that is black or deep blue in colour would be considered a dark god or goddess, that represents *dark matter*. I can readily think of Lord Krishna (or 'Shyam' which means 'black in Sanskrit), Goddess Kali (or 'Shyama' – feminine of 'Shyam') and Shiva Linga. Lord Jagannath is also one of the forms of Lord Krishna. Lord Krishna is the eighth *avatar* of Lord Vishnu who is dark blue/blue-grey/or black-skinned. Lord Rama (Raghubir) is also dark-skinned.

Dark masculine energy is the embodiment of a raw, unfiltered, masculine energy often associated with drive, assertiveness, resilience and unapologetic ambition. *Dark masculinity* is a sovereign entity, confident, untamed, and unswayed by societal norms. It coexists with empathy, compassion and vulnerability resulting in a balanced, holistic expression that is empowering and authentic.

The *Fair* (or, *light*) *masculine energy* is also known as the *divine masculine energy* that comes down through the *Sahasrar* or the *Crown Chakra*. It is full of higher truth, guidance, support, protection, and divine love for the feminine.

The *Dark feminine energy* is an embodiment of authenticity – an energy that transcends the superficial layers of societal expectations and dives into the rich reservoir of the self. It is a beckoning call to shed the masks imposed by society and embrace the genuine, pure self. It invites individuals to peel away the layers of conformity and connect with the raw authentic essence that resides within. *Dark feminine energy* is often associated with the sacred darkness – the womb of creation and transformation. This energy holds the potential for rebirth and renewal. Goddess Kali is a perfect example of *dark feminine energy.*

White (or *light*) or *divine* or *fair feminine energy* is being patient, elegant, forgiving, nurturing, playful and innocent. This energy rises up the *chakras* from the Earth. It is very grounding, soothing, nourishing, and naturally energizing. Sri Radhika is a perfect example of this type of *feminine energy.*

An ungrounded man will use women to ground himself. This is the *dark masculine.* On the other hand, the *divine masculine* is fully grounded to the Earth which allows him to stay relaxed under all circumstances. When we ground ourselves, our emotions can move down and out of our bodies to be taken by our Earth mother. This is why Lord Chaitanya Mahaprabhu, Sri Sri Ramakrishna, and the Sufi mystics roll on the ground when they are extra-ecstatic. Possibly also, this is the reason why Lord Shiva had laid his body on the ground to get rid of his negative emotions that had crowded in his mind finding Goddess Kali in a most fierce 'killer' mood. (References 33–37)

Human Genome and Dark Matter

When geneticists embarked on the Human Genome Project in the early 1990s, they had expected that one human being's 'gene pool' (that is, *genome*) would have the bulk of it comprising protein-coding *active* genes. Unfortunately, they were proven wrong. In April 2003, when the project came to an end, it was found that humans had only around 20,000 to 25,000 protein-coding genes which was equivalent to what the simplest creatures like ordinary worms had (even a fruit fly had 13,000). This was merely 2% of the whole genome, the remaining 98% was regarded as 'junk' without any specific function or purpose. Only now, the scientists are speculating that this bulk would be our genome's *dark matter* – the function of which is not easily understood, like the *dark matter* of the universe. They feel that this *dark genome* is crucial to understanding the vast human potential that is lying dormant, unutilised, being the product of millions of years of evolution facing, passing through and coping with so many different types of environmental circumstances. The *dark genome's* primary function appears to be regulating the decoding process, or expression, of protein-making genes. It helps to control how our genes behave in response to all the environmental pressures our bodies face throughout our lives, ranging from diet to stress, pollution, exercise, and how much we sleep, a field known as *epigenetics.*

An analogy: Imagine a library with billions of books, but the only books you read are the ones by Shakespeare.

The Super-genius Genome of an *Avatar*

The *dark human genome* offers me enough scope for speculation of the 'Super-genius Genome' of an *Avatar.*

An *Avatar Soul* is one who resides in one of the highest layers of the 'Post-death Realm' where there is only *dark matter* (made up of invisible, imperceptible particles) and *dark energy.* So, the *Avatar Soul* has no gross body. It manifests itself through different forms of energy and even, in one soul, the form of energy expressed may vary from time to time and may change from one situation to another. Nevertheless, when the *Avatar Soul* has to descend on earth, it has to have a 'gross body' made up of *genes.* Wherefrom such *genes* will come?

Let us take Sri Sri Ramakrishna's case.

His father Kshudiram had acquired *dark energy* from Gadadhar Lord Vishnu as Vishnu had told him explicitly that he would be born into his family as his son. A God does not choose a rich prosperous family to be born into as He is already from a super-rich background. He would like to experience a pure, humble, hand-to-mouth type of environment which is full of divine, spiritual vibes. Kshudiram's family environment just fitted with this requirement of Lord Vishnu. Kshudiram's entire biology was thus full of *dark energy* which came from the dark God Vishnu. His entire reproductive system, his testes, his semen, his sperms were brimming with *dark energy* – ready to contribute *dark genes* to the foetus. Same was the case with Ramakrishna's mother Chandramani. She had acquired *dark energy* from the dark God Shiva and her reproductive system also, her ovaries, her uterus, vagina, ova were all full of *dark energy*. Her vagina thus represented a *black hole* ready to suck the semen from her husband's genital organ to make the fusion between his sperm and her ovum to form a zygote having *super-genius genome*.

An *Avatar Soul* likes to descend under a circumstance when all conditions are satisfied to receive such a soul to form a zygote *having a super-genius genome*. And that is exactly what happened in the case of Gadadhar's (later known as 'Ramakrishna') birth. The family deity was also Raghubir – Lord Rama, a dark *avatar* of Lord Vishnu. So, the Chattopadhyay household was full of *dark energy* vibe. It represented a *mini cosmos*. (References 38–43)

References

[1] Gianfranco Bertone and Dan Hooper, "How dark matter became a particle", *CERNCOURIER,* 13th April 2017.

[2] "New Clues About the Nature of Dark Energy: Einstein May Have Been Right After All", *NASA Hubblesite,* 20th February 2004.

[3] "NASA's Hubble Traces Dark Matter in Dwarf Galaxy Using Stellar Motions", *NASA,* NASA Hubble Mission team, Goddard Space Flight Centre, 11th July 2024.

[4] "Dark Matter and Dark Energy explained by Dareld Gillaspie", YouTube Video Presentation.

[5] Siddhartha Ganguli, *The Third Eye: The Mystery of Sri Sri Ramakrishna's Visions,* Noida: Allied Publishers Pvt. Ltd., 2024.

[6] Dr Brian Weiss, *Many Lives, Many Masters,* London: Piatkus, 1994.

[7] "Beyond the Big Bang: The Ancient Theory of Creation/*Nasadiya Sukta*" Video Presentation on YouTube, Bharat Verse Channel.

[8] "What Is Higgs Boson And Why It Is Called 'The God Particle'", *NDTV*, 10th April 2024.

[9] "SN Bose: Physicist par excellence and forgotten 'Father of God Particle'", *India Science, Technology and Innovation Portal*

[10] "All the evidence we have for a dark matter/A century's worth of science history", Video Presentation on You Tube, Dr Becky's Channel.

[11] Parashuram Chitale, "Is it true that everything in the universe was created from the energy of pure love from a higher power? If so, why do some things in the world possess negative energy instead of positive energy?" *Quora* https://www,quora.com.

[12] "DOE Explains..........Dark Matter", US Department of Energy, Office of Science.

[13] "How do we know how much dark matter there is in the universe?" YouTube Video Presentation, Dr Becky's Channel.

[14] "The legendary discovery of black holes: The Day Tomorrow Began": Big Brains Podcast, Video Presentation on You Tube, University of Chicago, UChicago Podcast Network.

[15] "Subrahmanyan Chandrasekhar's Contributions and His Life", unacademy.com.

[16] "Hearts of Darkness: Black Holes in Space", Video Presentation in You Tube, by Dr Alex Filipenko, University of California, Berkeley, 19th May 2010.

[17] "Black Holes: The End of Time or a New Beginning?" SV Astronomy Lectures, Video Presentation on You Tube by Dr Roger Blandford of Kavli Institute for Particle Astrophysics & Cosmology, Stanford University, 19th March 2013.

[18] "What If a White Hole and Black Hole Collided?" Video Presentation on YouTube, 'What If' Channel.

[19] "What Happens When a White Hole and a Black Hole Collide?" Video Presentation on You Tube, Action Lab Channel.

[20] Adam Mann, "Dark energy from supermassive black holes? Physicists spar over radical idea" *Science*, 17th February 2023.

[21] Robert Lea, "Black holes that form in 'reverse Big Bang replays' could account for dark energy" *SPACE.com*, 2nd November 2024.

[22] Hayley Dunning, "Scientists find first evidence that black holes are the source of dark energy", *Imperial News*, 15th February 2023.

[23] "Shocking: Are Black Holes the Source of Dark Energy? New Evidence!" Video Presentation on You Tube, *NASA Space News Channel.*

[24] "Black Holes and Dark Energy: A Cosmic History" with Dr. Chris Pearson, STFC, *Friends of Imperial College Channel*, 30th June 2023.

[25] "Neem Karoli Baba" – *Wikipedia.*

[26] "Ram Dass" – *Wikipedia.*

[27] "Krishna Das" – *Wikipedia.*

[28] "Raphael Mechoulam" – *Wikipedia.*

[29] "Lumir Ondrej Hanus" – *Wikipedia*

[30] "Anandamide" – *Wikipedia.*

[31] T.L. Dunlop, "Exploring Anandamide: The Bliss Molecule in Our Bodies", *Essentially Healthy Living*, 12th November 2023.

[32] Maria Scherma *et al.*, "Brain activity of anandamide: a rewarding bliss?" *Acta Pharmacologica Sinica*, 2019, Vol. 40, pp. 309–323.

[33] Joa White Eagle, "The Dark Masculine vs the Divine Masculine", I AM University, iam-university.org.

[34] Helia Sarigul, "What Is Dark Feminine Energy, Best Explained in 5 Steps", *Goddess*, 19th December 2023.

[35] "How to Unlock Your Dark Masculinity", Video Presentation on You Tube, Gent Z Channel.

[36] "How to master dark masculinity", Video Presentation on You Tube, The Update Channel.

[37] "Lord Vishnu" – *Wikipedia.*

[38] David Cox, "The mystery of the human genome's dark matter", *BBC*, 13th April 2023.

[39] Kelly Rae Chi, "The dark side of the human genome", *nature*, 2016, 538, pp. 275–277.

[40] Alfred Grech and Michael Balzan, "The Matter of the Genome: Some Insights and Clinical Applications, *The Synapse.net*, 2016, Vol. 15, Issue 03, pp. 7–9. (L-Universita ta Malta).

[41] Ibrahim Bozgeyik, "The dark matter of the human genome and its role in human cancers", *Science Direct* (*Gene*), Vol. 811, 15th February 2022, 146084.

[42] Anthony J. Hannan, "Tandem Repeats and Repeatomes: Delving Deeper into the 'Dark Matter' of Genomes", *EBioMedicine*, 2018, Vol. 31, pp. 3–4.

[43] "Genome 'dark matter'" *EUPROFILE*, University of Copenhagen, Denmark.

PART TWO

Two Super Souls – Spiritual

Sri Krishna Chaitanya Mahaprabhu
(1486–1534)
(The Dark God Sri Krishna)

Sri Sri Ramakrishna
(1836–1886)
(The Dark Goddess Kali)

Sri Krishna Chaitanya Mahaprabhu

Sri Sri Ramakrishna

CHAPTER 3

Sri Krishna Chaitanya Mahaprabhu

Sri Chaitanya: Whose Reincarnation and in What Form

Lord Krishna, a major deity in Hinduism, is worshipped as the eighth *avatar* of Lord Vishnu and also as the Supreme God in his own right. He is the god of protection, compassion, tenderness, and love.

He was very fond of the Yamuna River as the earlier period of his life was spent in Vrindavan through which Yamuna flows. Once he was bathing playfully with his friends and loved ones in the Yamuna. Seeing this, Mother Ganga went straight to Lord Vishnu and started mourning: "Oh, Lord, I'm so close to you and my origin and source are from your lotus feet. But still I have never got a chance to be of any service to you, while you in the form of Sri Krishna do have so much fun in the water of Yamuna which is not so wide and deep as I am."

Lord Vishnu replied: "Don't you worry! Very soon, I in my Sri Krishna form along with my most favourite consort Sri Radhika would take birth in *Gour Banga* (the old name of Bengal), and will spend a lot of time with you". In due course, Sri Radha Madhav was born as Biswambhar Misra (home name – Nimai) who later became Bhagawan Sri Chaitanya Mahaprabhu. Nimai swam and bathed, every day, in the water of the Holy River Ganges right from his childhood to adolescence. He was an ace swimmer. The Holy water of Ganges loved and felt blessed to be in touch with the well-proportioned body of Nimai who was very tall and most handsome with a golden skin, radiating a high vibrational aura around him.

When Sri Krishna was about to return to Vaikuntha Dham, all his friends, Gopis, Brajabasis, and the whole of Vrindavan started shedding tears. Sri Krishna took the mournful Sri Radhika aside and said:

> "I don't want to miss you Radhike, so I've to devise a strategy by which both of us would descend on earth in a form so that nobody can identify us." Taken by surprise, Sri Radhika asked: "What will our goal be in the material world?" Prompt came Sri Krishna's reply. He said: "The Kali Yuga has already commenced and there are conflicts, widespread violence, destructions, lies and deceit – leading to misinterpretations of my *Gita*, impacting the religious practices severely. So, I have decided to reincarnate not as God but in the form of his most *devoted* devotee."

Actually, what Sri Krishna had in mind is this: Sri Radha was the most *devoted* devotee of Sri Krishna. Her devotion was unparalleled; and *love* of the most *devoted* devotee is the highest and purest. It had nothing to do with physical love. But unfortunately, Sri Krishna could not get the *feel* of the true nature of that pure unconditional love. So, he wanted to experience himself, first hand, the love that Sri Radhika had for him. He descended in 1486 in Nabadwip, Gour Banga, located on the bank of the Holy River Ganges, as Biswambhar, our beloved Gouranga, (nickname *Nimai*) as the combination of the twin forms of Sri Krishna and Sri Radhika. He took the gender from Sri Krishna and the colour and texture of the skin and the mood (*bhava*) brimming with pure love, compassion, kindness and mercy from Sri Radhika. Together, they later became Bhagawan Sri Krishna Chaitanya Mahaprabhu who represented *prema avatar*, brimming with the love-compassion-empathy-bonding-and-trust molecule *Oxytocin.* (References 1–6)

The Twin-Souled *Avatar*

"Radha and Krishna both
are your most beloved ones
You have both
their souls inside you
Ray says: Oh, My Lord!
Please take off your pretences
Do not steal and hide
your real identity from me!!"

(Ray Ramananda, Vaishnava poet Originally in Bengali, translated into English by me) (References 7 & 8)

The main protagonist of the Gaudiya Vaishnava cult was Sri Krishna Chaitanya Mahaprabhu (1486–1534). He was born as a male, but his soul was a balanced mixture of Bhagawan Sri Krishna and his principal consort Sri Radha, as in conduct and behaviour he used to display both the characters. It was he who restored the almost-extinct Vaishnava cult. And, although some controversy still exists, he reformed it to a large extent from the *tantric sahajiya* form, and re-established it on a very sound and solid footing with the help of his myriads of disciples, devotees and admirers. He was enunciated by Iswarpuri Goswami who was the direct disciple of the most reputed and respected man in the study and practice of the Radha-Krishna principles Madhavendra Puri Goswami. Iswarpuri is regarded as the seed of the Gaudiya Vaishnava cult. Sri Chaitanya Mahaprabhu can be compared to its solid trunk and his two main disciples Advaita and Nityananda they are the two main branches. There are millions of disciples and devotees who can be regarded as the myriads of smaller branches, twigs and leaves. Although Chaitanya Dev had never had the good fortune of meeting Madhavendra Puri as he left his mortal body when Chaitanya was a very small boy, later he used to chant four lines from a verse composed by Madhavendra and get into ecstasy. The essence of those four lines is: "Oh, Kind-hearted Soul! Oh, My Lord!, Oh the King of Mathura! When shall I have the good fortune of having your *darshan* and getting your blessings personally?"

The main contribution of Sri Chaitanya and his followers was their thrust on the *madhura bhava* in the spiritual world. It was highlighted by Bhagawan Sri Krishna's *Vrindavan Leela,* without which Vrindavan would have remained as a mere forest. It was Sri Chaitanya who had rediscovered Vrindavan and established the right significance of *Sri Krishna Leela.*

Incidentally, Madhavendra Puri used to lose his consciousness on witnessing *dark* clouds on the sky, just in the same way as Sri Radhika used to respond to the sight of dark clouds.

Sri Chaitanya's love had no bounds. The saint or the sinner, the Hindu or the Muslim, the rich or the poor, the pure or the impure, the prostitute, the destitute, the streetwalker – all had a share in his love;

all had a share in his mercy and forgiveness. And, even to the present day, his sect is the refuge of the poor, or the downtrodden, of the outcast, of the weak, of those, who have been rejected by the society. (References 9)

Lord Vishnu

The *Vedas* were scripted during the period of about 1500–1200 BCE. In the Vedic age, there were three main Gods: Brahma, Vishnu, and Maheswara.

According to the *Rig Veda*, Lord Vishnu was one form of the Sun. He was dressed in the Sun's rays; and with the help of those rays, he used to cover, protect and light up the entire world of ours. I am indeed intrigued to find such significant reference of astronomy in the religious scriptures. In several other verses of the *Rig Veda*, Lord Vishnu has been shown as *Aditya* or 'Sun'. Vishnu is providing life-force to the entire universe through his solar rays. He is the protector. He is the God of permanence.

Again, in the *Puranas*, we find the ten (10) *avatars* of Vishnu Bhagawan. One of those *avatars* is the *Vamana avatar* – the 'dwarf' incarnate. Amongst the three steps of the *Vamana avatar*, two are earthly. His third step is Vishnu's *Great Step* (*'Param Pad'*) which is placed very high up, much beyond the material and physical world, much beyond the human perception and imagination; much beyond the reach of the high-flying birds. That is where there is eternal *bliss*. Most pious souls reach that space after they leave their mortal body on this planet. Now, after so many centuries, '*Vishnu Pad*' means the whole firmament. And, by *'Vishnu Lok'* it is meant the place high up into the space above, much beyond the sky that is visible to us, where the sacred souls reside after death. Lord Vishnu has been described and his attributes and personality traits have been portrayed in various ways in the ancient scriptures. Those who worship Lord Vishnu are known as *Vaishnavas*.

One comes across the name of Bhagawan Vasudeva or Krishna for the first time in Srimad Bhagavad Gita. He is considered inseparable from Lord Vishnu. In the epic *Mahabharata*, and in many of the ancient *Puranas*, Vasudeva Krishna has been shown as the main Hindu God and propagator of the *Bhakti* cult. The religion practised by the Vaishnavas is thus known as the *Bhagavad Dharma*.

Bhagawan Vishnu had mentioned once that whenever *dharma* will be contaminated and overpowered by *adharma*, he will appear on this planet as the protector and preserver of true religion. With that objective, he had descended as Lord Rama in the *Treta Yuga* and as Lord Krishna in the *Dwapara Yuga* to save true religion from the hands of the sinners.

Bhagawan Sri Krishna

In ancient times, there was a king by the name of Kangsasur who used to be demonic in character. He used to torture his subjects too much, but they were helpless as Kangsasur had been blessed by Lord Shiva with a boon that he will die only in the hands of his own nephew who was yet to be born. Lord Brahma was sympathetic. He took a few of the gods to Lord Vishnu who was immersed in deep meditation. He requested Vishnu to take birth in the womb of Kangsa's sister Daibaki, and bring peace in the troubled land by killing King Kangsa.

Vishnu pondered for a little while and then requested Lord Shiva to allow Goddess Durga to accompany him to earth and assured him that she will return to heaven after a year. When Shiva agreed, Vishnu proceeded towards Mathura taking Devi Durga and his own wife Goddess Lakshmi along with him and descended in the house of Daibaki and her husband Basudeb in the baby form. The couple were at loss as how to protect the baby from the cruel hands of Kangsasur. Finding them so tensed, Vishnu appeared in front of them in his real form. He released Basudeb from the prison and he put the prison guards to deep sleep.

Just when Sri Krishna was born to Daibaki, a female child Jogmaya was born to Yashoda, the wife of Goparaj Nanda. Newborn Sri Krishna instructed Basudeb to take him secretly to Nanda's house and bring Jogmaya to Daibaki's house. Basudeb laid baby Krishna by the side of Yashoda and brought Jogmaya to Daibaki. Everything was done very secretly. On his return, Basudeb again entered into the prison and was locked up.

As Kangsasur got the news of the birth of the child, he arrived at the prison and found his sister Daibaki was holding the baby to her chest. Without listening to her request, Kangsa snatched the child and threw it on a huge piece of stone. Most amazingly, the baby, instead of falling on the stone, started moving upwards and finally took the form of the goddess with eight hands. The goddess said to Kangsa: "There is no end to your misdeeds. The child who will kill you is growing in the land of the cowherds." The goddess now returned to her husband Lord Shiva on Mount Kailas. The story of the birth of Lord Krishna has been described and documented in the *Puranas* exactly in this manner.

The Dark God Sri Krishna

'Krishna' is a Sanskrit word, which means 'black' or 'dark' or 'dark bluish'. It also means 'the attractive'.

On his return from Chicago, Swami Vivekananda went to Madras College for giving lectures to the students there. During his lecture, he asked a question to the students present: "Why Bhagawan Sri Krishna's skin colour is dark blue?"

Many boys tried but their answers did not satisfy Swamiji. Finally, one boy stood up and said: "Sri Krishna was dark bluish in colour because he has all the cosmic powers that the universe has." The boy was C. Rajagopalachari – former governor general of India.

Krishna's skin colour was bluish black like the rain-bearing cloud, which has a dual nature. As long as the cloud does not burst into heavy showers, storm, lightning and thunder, it is very pleasant as it cools up the environment. The moment it becomes outraged and furious, it can turn into a cyclone uprooting plants and trees. In the same way, there is a difference between the nature of Sri Krishna of Vrindaban and Sri Krishna of Mathura. The former is an embodiment of love, compassion and *Madhur Rasa* whereas the latter is a symbol of wealth and courage. The Sri Krishna of Mathura is the King, who establishes his power and authority using his sharp multi-faceted intelligence. Vrindaban is heavenly – there is no opportunity there for exercise of power and authority. Krishna thus has a dual personality – one with the brain bathed by the love-compassion-trust molecule *'Oxytocin'* (*'O'*), typical of a kind and considerate female; and, the other having abundance of the male sex hormone *'Testosterone'* (*'T'*) released in the blood.

However, in Vrindavan also, in very exceptional cases, Sri Krishna exercised his power and authority if needed. I will share one such case here. There is the river Yamuna in Vrindavan. A most poisonous snake Kaliya used to live in Yamuna. It used to secrete its poison in the river so that no living creature – even birds and wild beasts could bathe or swim in or drink the river water. Kaliya's poison was so strong that no plant or tree could grow on the river bank. There was only one Kadamba tree standing alone. Kaliya's only enemy was Garuda who, incidentally, was cursed by a powerful Yogi that its death was inevitable if it had visited Vrindavan ever.

The villagers were scared about Kaliya and the river water was of no use for them. When Sri Krishna became aware of this predicament of the villagers, he jumped into the river, located Kaliya and started dancing on each of his multiple hoods leading to its breakage. Finding Kaliya in great distress, its many wives came and started praying to Sri Krishna so that he stopped his wild-style dance. By then, Kaliya had lost consciousness and most of its multiple hoods were damaged.

Then, slowly when Kaliya regained consciousness, most humbly it said to Sri Krishna: "Sir! We, members of the snake species are very negative-minded from birth itself. We are extremely aggressive by nature. And, I simply do not know how I can change my natural propensity. And, since you are the Creator, you do whatever you want to do. I've nothing to say. You have infused poison in me, wherefrom can I get the nectar?"

Sri Krishna was very firm. He said: "Vrindavan is inhabited by many *sadhus*. The Yamuna River is of no utility for them. So, you have to restrain yourself. You can make the river your home but do not release your poison into the river water. Your poison has to be used most restrictively for your self-defence."

How Lord Krisna's *Dark Energy* Had Helped Jayadeva

Gita Gobinda is a classical work by the 12th century Hindu poet from Bengal, *Jayadeva*. It describes the relationship between Krishna, Radha, and the *gopis* (female cow herders) of Vrindavan. The original verses were written on palm leaf.

Every night in the Puri Jagannath temple, the *Gita Govinda* is sung in the style of Odisi music, a tradition that has continued unbroken since the time of *Jayadeva* himself. Musicians of Kerala have adapted some portions of *Gita Govinda* into a musical form performed in temples called *sopana sangeetham*. *Jayadeva*'s hymns are also included in the *Guru Grantha Sahib*.

Jayadeva used to worship Sri Krishna and Radha together. Since Radha was completely filled with love-rich devotion for Krishna, *Jayadeva* had acquired *dark energy* from both of them.

Most interestingly, while writing about Krishna's begging by touching Radha's feet to appease her, the poet failed to write anything. His pen stopped as he felt most embarrassed to make the God touch a milk-maid's feet.

Finding this, Bhagawan Sri Krishna himself entered into *Jayadeva*'s body in the subtle form (it wasn't difficult as the poet already had *dark energy*) and prompted him to write it. He then took lunch from the poet's wife *Padmavati* without anybody knowing about his presence.

He was invisible. (References 8 & 10)

God as *Black Hole*

God has no meaningful existence without god-believers and god-lovers. He is no God unless He has the ability to suck them up as *black holes*. Similarly, *avatars* (who are *godmen*) like Bhagawan Sri Krishna Chaitanya or Sri Sri Ramakrishna are meaningless unless they are able influence people with spiritual potential and attract really devoted devotees who are prepared to lead a life of total surrender without any hesitation.

Mahaprabhu Sri Chaitanya used to chant, sing and dance to the tune of *hare krishna nam*, brimming with pure unconditional love and devotion. While dancing, he used to fall down and roll on the ground in total ecstasy. In this process, he will lose his golden lustre and his whole body will be full of dust and dirt.

Once one young celibate *brahmachari* was very keen to witness Sri Chaitanya's *harinam sankirtan*, combined with dance. This young brahmin used to follow all the religious rituals meticulously and had thought that it was good enough to move close to the Godhead. With that desire in mind, he had once approached Chaitanyadev's associate Sribas who agreed but set a condition that he will be allowed to witness Chaitanyadev's *leela* from a distance only and he should not be seen by the *avatar*.

Sri Chaitanya was singing and dancing in his typical style of *madhura bhava* but suddenly he stopped and said: "I am not able to get into the right mood today. I'm getting very much disturbed and distracted and am not able to concentrate on the *hari nam*. Has any stranger entered the house?" Sribas told him the truth about the presence of the young celibate brahmin. This outraged Sri Chaitanya and he asked Sribas to drive the young man out. He said: "Only a highly disciplined life and celibacy do not help one to attain God's grace. What one requires is – unstinted devotion (*bhakti*). There must be total yearning for God like a child cries for its mother and stops crying only when the mother takes it on her lap." The young brahmin listened attentively and could realise where he was going wrong, where he was lacking. The sudden change in his attitude could be felt by Bhagawan Sri Krishna Chaitanya who called him in and started explaining to him how one can get God's direct blessings. He emphasized that penance and ritualistic lifestyle were not enough one must have the spirit of total surrender (which means the devotee must allow God to suck him entirely just like a *black hole* in the space).

The whole of Nabadwip got the news of the transformation of the young brahmachari and the inhabitants became interested in chanting and singing *hari nam* in a rhythmic style. Town and rural folks came out of their houses and started chanting and dancing. This crowd included members of the lowest castes, beggars and destitutes who earlier used to be unloved, hated and totally neglected by the rich and wealthy and also by those belonging to the higher castes.

Bhagawan Sri Krishna Chaitanya's Childhood Sport (*Leela*)

Little Chaitanya was given the name *Biswambhar* (home name – *Nimai*) during the customary naming ceremony.

In his childhood, no signs of his later *avatarhood* were manifested as he had most naughty behaviour like any other boy of his age. Many of his childhood sports (*leela*) used to take place in the water of the Holy River Ganges when he used to take bath for up to late afternoon every day.

These included: touching someone with a dirty hand who had to have a wash once again in a most upset mood; sprinkling water on one who was meditating in half-deep water; snatching the little *deity* (bal gopal or shiv ling) from someone who had brought it for giving a bath in the Holy river water; shifting the *dhoti* or *banian* of a bather to a different place from where he had put it originally; pulling someone's leg under water; putting some adhesive seed inside the hair of female bathers.

Nimai's misdeeds on the ground included: eating the *prasad* or *bhog* before it was offered to the deity; hiding fruits or flowers and other offerings in order to create confusion; eating up food cooked up by *sannyasis* visiting Nimai's home.

Note: These were Nimai's various childlike ways of earning the 'feel good' neurotransmitter *'Dopamine'* (*'D'*). (Reference 11)

The first sprout of the desire tree of devotion towards Bhagawan Sri Krishna was manifested in the monk Madhavendra Puri. That sprout developed into a sapling in the person of the monk Isvara Puri, who was Madhavendra's disciple. Isvara Puri had met Nimai in Gaya and Nimai was so impressed with him that he requested Isvara Puri to be his guru. Eventually, after some years, when Isvara Puri enunciated him, the sapling of devotion became the trunk of an enormous tree – the desire tree of devotion.

Sri Chaitanya Mahaprabhu: A Combination of Lord Sri Krishna and Sri Radhika

The deep urge of Sri Radharani for Bhagawan Sri Krishna is beautifully expressed through the following song (translated by me from the Bengali folk song by Fakir Lalan Shah):

"For how long must I wait
to be united with 'The Man of My Heart'?
Throughout the day and night,
the swallow stares at the dark moon
with its hidden desire to serve like a slave
Just like the lightning that hides between the layers
of the cloud, visible only to those longing to see!
The same way, I see the dark God in my mind's mirror
hidden from the public gaze.
When I envision his form crystal clear,
I throw away my veil of shame and run to be
united with him
Fakir Lalan thinks, feels and says always:
Only the person who LOVES,
would know, no one else!!"

The *Brihadaranyaka Upanishad* says that *Purusha* splits himself up into two parts, male and female and the two halves copulate, producing all life – a theme concurrent in *Ardhanarishvara*'s tales. In our universe, we exist within light and darkness. We experience hot and cold. We also live within the duality of energy known as 'masculine' and 'feminine'. The physical world and our bodily experience as well as our emotions (positive and negative) are located within this *duality*. GOD has masculine and feminine energy within Him in a well-proportioned, balanced manner.

Lord Sri Krishna is the reservoir of all pleasure, and Sri Radhika is the personification of ecstatic love of Godhead. These two forms had combined as one in Sri Chaitanya Mahaprabhu. Mahaprabhu revealed his real form to Ramananda Raya.

Upon seeing this form, Ramananda Raya lost consciousness in transcendental bliss. When he fell to the ground, Chaitanya Dev touched his hand, and he immediately regained consciousness. But when he saw Lord Chaitanya in the dress of a *sannyasi*, he was struck with wonder. After embracing Ramananda, the Lord pacified him by saying: "But for you, no one has ever seen me in this form."

Ramananda responded by saying: "My dear Lord, I can understand that You have assumed the ecstasy and bodily complexion of Srimati Radharani. By accepting this, You are tasting Your own personal transcendental humour and have therefore appeared as Sri Chaitanya Mahaprabhu. At the same time, You are transforming the whole world by spreading the ecstasy of love of Godhead."

I am tempted to share another beautiful Baul song by the songwriters Din Sarat and Radharaman Dutta both from Bangladesh (earlier from undivided Bengal) (translation into English mine):

"Oh, My Lord Banamali
In Your next birth, please do
come as Radha!!
Like me, do experience
charcoal fire burning deep
in Your heart!
Like me, wear a garland
of separation anxiety
And go to the bank of the
Holy River Yamuna
Despite the warning of Your kin
and folks!
Oh, My Lord, Banamali
In Your next birth, please do
come as Radha!
Like me, let tears roll down
Your cheeks from both
Your eyes

Only then, You may realise
what pains Radha had to bear
without You by her side!
You suffer like me with grievous
thoughts leaving no vacant
space in Your mind!

Think what Sarat is saying to Krishna
Tie me up in the chain of love.
Once I die, I will be Lord Krishna
And shall make You, my Radha!!"

The Mystery of the Tota Gopinath Temple

The Tota Gopinath Temple at Jagannath Dham, Puri is one of the places that carries the mystery of Sri Krishna Chaitanya Dev's sudden disappearance into oblivion.

After 5,000 years of *Kali Yuga* had elapsed, Lord Krishna along with Srimati Radharani had incarnated as Chaitanya Mahaprabhu. The mission of the Lord was to initiate the chanting of the Holy names of Krishna as the only means of deliverance in the *Kali Yuga*. Lord Chaitanya Mahaprabhu had made Jagannath Dham Puri as His primeval seat for preaching Vaishnavism.

Once in Jagannath Dham Puri, Sri Chaitanya Mahaprabhu became so overwhelmed with the love of Lord Krishna, that he began searching for him everywhere around. The nearby sand dunes of Chataka Parvat appeared to him like the Govardhan Hill and the sea flowing to be the Holy Yamuna River. In ecstasy, Mahaprabhu started digging the sand and he suddenly found a stone image of Lord Krishna. He named it as Gopinath and as it was found in a 'Tota' (meaning 'garden'), it came to be known as *Tota Gopinath*. He entrusted the worship of the image to his dearest disciple – Sri Gadadhar Pandit who, it is said, was the incarnation of Srimati Radharani.

Originally, the image of Tota Gopinath was in a standing posture in the *tribhangi* form – his body bent at three planes or places. Later the deity adopted a sitting posture as Sri Gadadhar Pandit used to face difficulty in worshipping his tall figure.

After manifesting his physical sport (*leela*) for forty-eight years, Chaitanya Mahaprabhu concluded his *avatar* existence in the world. One day, while the *kirtan* singing was going on in the *Tota Gopinath* Temple, Sri Chaitanya was dancing in deep ecstasy. He then suddenly entered the altar of the *Tota Gopinath* image and disappeared permanently. The spot where Mahaprabhu had disappeared into the Deity is still visible as a golden line of Lord *Tota Gopinath*.

There are three altars within the *Tota Gopinath* Temple. On the central altar, one can have *darshan* of Sri *Tota Gopinath* along with the deities Srimati Radharani and Lalita, respectively on the left and the right sides of *Gopinath*. Radharani holds a *veena* and Lalita a *bansuri*. The most interesting fact is that both *Radharani and Lalita are 'black' ('dark' in complexion) as they are engrossed in the thoughts of the Dark God Krishna*. (Reference 12)

Sri Chaitanya Mahaprabhu Losing His 'Body Consciousness'

In the Presence of Dark Matter

Lord Jagannath of Puri Dham is a *dark* God. Sri Chaitanya Mahaprabhu used to lose his 'body consciousness' whenever he used to be looking at Jagannath's image inside the Puri temple. I will share one such incident.

Sri Chaitanya Dev used to wake up every morning by the sound of the conch shell being blown inside the Jagannath temple in Puri. Thereafter, he used to get ready to visit the temple for *darshan*. And, most amazingly, the moment he stepped into the temple premises, his mental frame used to take an internal turn. His mind will be shut to all external stimuli and he used to lose even his body consciousness. It will get immersed in the thought of Lord Jagannath. He used to stand supporting his body on the Garuda column lest he would become totally unmindful about his body and fall down. Sometimes, tears of deep devotion would roll down both his cheeks. At some other times, he would be so much absorbed in divine thoughts (a kind of '*bhav samadhi*') that he will stand like a stone statue. Lay people simply could not make out if it was a living being or a statue made of clay or stone.

Like this, one day, he was standing like a statue leaning his body on the Garuda column. The temple was overcrowded on that day. People were struggling to get a good *darshan* of Lord Jagannath. Around that time, a local village woman came close to him, desirous of having a *darshan*. She mistook Sri Chaitanya to be a solid pillar and climbed up on his shoulder to get a good view. She was not conscious of what she was doing; and Chaitanya Dev, on his part, was also not in his normal senses – he was so much absorbed in the glory of the *dark matter* of which the deity was made. And, Jagannath's darkness was most prominent in contrast with the fair Balaram and Subhadra on his either side.

After a little while, a *sevak* of Sri Chaitanya, by the name of Gobinda arrived and he was wonder-struck at that scene. He moved forward to pull that woman down. Mahaprabhu came to his normal senses for a little while and prevented him quietly from touching the woman. However, the woman would have become conscious of what she was doing. So, she came down and fell at Chaitanya's feet seeking his forgiveness. However, the *avatar* was not annoyed at all. Instead, he started praising her for her pure devotion.

Such was Sri Chaitanya! In the presence of the *dark deity,* he would get into the 'Flow Brain State' ('FBS') and lose the sense of time, place, space, and 'self' (own body and mind). It is an 'Altered State of Consciousness' ('ASC'), so typical of spiritually highly advanced people.

To quote the words of Swami Vivekananda: "The stone on which Chaitanya used to stand in the temple of Jagannatha to see the image was worn by his tears of love and devotion. When he took Sannyasa, he showed his fitness for it to his Guru by keeping sugar on his tongue for some time without it being dissolved."

A Devotional Song That Reminded Me of Sri Chaitanya's Surrender to the Dark God

"All that I am, all that I have
I lay them down before You, O Lord
All my regrets, all my acclaim
the joy and the pain. I'm making them Yours.
Lord, I offer my life to You
Everything I've been through
Use it for Your glory
Lord, I offer my days to You
Lifting my praise to You, as a pleasing sacrifice.
Lord, I offer You my life
Things in the past, things yet unseen
Wishes and dreams that are yet to come true!
All my hopes, all my plans
My heart and my hand are lifted to You,
Lord, I offer my life to You
Everything I've been through
Use it for Your glory
Lord, I offer my days to You,
Lifting my praise to You, as a pleasing sacrifice!
Lord, I offer You my life
Lord, I offer You my life!!"

(Lyrics & Song by Don Moen, 1950-born American singer, pianist and songwriter, specializing in Christian worship music)

Tales about Sri Chaitanya's Disappearance into Oblivion

There are quite a few such tales. I suppose, mostly speculations because nobody had ever reported of having had been the only spectator of how the godman's life had come to an end. The most popular tale is the one that I'm going to narrate now. Since I am investigating about *dark matter* and *dark energy* now, this version appeals to me most.

For the last quite a few years of his life, Mahaprabhu had been settled in the Jagannath Dham Puri as he was passionately in spiritual love with the *Neela Madhava* – the dark god Lord Jagannath. The God's deep bluish black skin colour used to draw him towards the deity like a powerful magnet. The *dark matter* used to radiate most *'attractive'* (another meaning of *'krishna'*) *dark energy.*

For twenty-four long years, Chaitanya never used to enter into the *Garbha Griha* of the Puri Jagannath temple. Instead, he used to have *darshan* by standing by the side of the *Garuda Column.* And, because he could not touch the base where the deities' images were installed, he used to shed tears most profusely. One day, when he felt that his end was near, he entered into the *Garbha Griha* absolutely alone; the main door got shut and he could not resist the temptation of running suddenly towards the Jagannath image and touch it with his own fingers. While he looked ceaselessly into the *dark* eyes of the *dark* deity, he lost his senses. He went into *samadhi.* At that very instant, a dark blue ray of light came out of Lord Jagannath's *dark* body, encircled him and sucked him into the *dark* body of the deity. The behaviour of the image was just like the *black holes* up above in the cosmic space. (*Black holes suck anything that comes in their vicinity and white holes behave in just the opposite manner – they eject*). In other words, the *avatar* got a place in the heart of his most beloved God. This version is also acceptable to a group of the Vaishnavites; they do not express any doubt. As nobody witnessed this incident, the conclusion is entirely speculative. However, the speculation appears to be sensible to me because, according to one version, the *avatar*'s lifeless body was lying in the temple room – so one can infer that his soul – the subtle body had merged into the deity. The other version which says that his body was not to be found anywhere and possibly he was taken in 'alive' or 'dead' condition through a secret underground passage to a far-away place and either buried or taken to a distant location. Since that place is close to the sea, one shouldn't be surprised if the body was washed away by the waves of the ocean. However, Chaitanya's body was not to be found anywhere in the nearby forest area also.

There is a most worldly version also which had been documented by his contemporary Vaishnava poet Jayananda. According to him, in the month of August, 1533, it was *Ratha Yatra* time. Sri Chaitanya Dev was leading the procession in front of the chariot and he was dancing to the rhythm of the kirtan. In the *bhava*, he had lost his 'body consciousness'. Suddenly, he fell down on the roadway and his left foot had struck on a piece of broken brick which was infested with the faeces of a horse. As a consequence, he had suffered a deep wound and it led to *tetanus*. The infection came from the horse faeces. On the third day of this accident, his pain increased a lot and he had very high fever. On the sixth day, he passed away. This most practical version of his death is not found acceptable to the staunch Vaishnavas as they think it is impossible for Bhagawan Sri Sri Chaitanya Dev as he was an *avatar* – a God incarnate who can end his earthly existence only by getting merged into the body of the deity. Orthodox Vaishnavas do not approve of poet Jayananda's *Chaitanya Mangal Kavya*'s version. Instead, they have acclaimed poet Vrindaban Das's *Chaitanya Mangal*, the title of which was changed to *Chaitanya Bhagavad*, as Chaitanya Dev was upgraded to the level of Lord Krishna as *Bhagavad* talks about Lord Krishna. It became much easier to perceive Chaitanya as an *avatar* of Lord Krishna.

[***Note:*** Please watch the concluding scene of the Hindi Movie *Shri Chaitanya Mahaprabhu*, starring Nitish Bharadwaj, Madhu and Saheb Chatterjee on YouTube in the 'Hindi Movies' Channel where Mahapradhu is being sucked into the Dark God Jagannath's body – a *black hole* phenomenon.]

Sri Chaitanya's Ecstasy in '*Madhura Bhava*'

The Vaishnavas believe in and also make it a point to practice five *bhavas: shanta* (tranquil & poised); *dasya* (spirit of service); *sakhya* (playful friendliness); *vatsalya* (compassion and affection); and, *madhura* or *madhurjya* (unconditional love without any desire). While in Nawadip, Mahaprabhu Sri Chaitanya used to spend all his time in the *madhura bhava*. That was his most favourite as he was a combination of male and female propensities. Physically he was male, but in spirit and soul, he was female. His devotees used to believe that he had descended as an *avatar* with that duality in him to demonstrate to common man the glory of the divine relationship between Sri Krishna and Sri Radhika, which was much beyond the earthly mundane physical plane. Mahaprabhu's fair skin represented *Sri Radhika.* It was just a cover to hide the *dark energy* present inside, representing Sri Krishna. Sea water appears dark and deep blue at a far-away distance, when you see it from near, it does not appear dark at all; on the contrary, the foam at the crest, make the waves look white.

Mahaprabhu used to lose his consciousness at times, being over-ecstatic. At some other times, his whole body would get stimulated with excitement. At times, he will perspire so heavily that it seemed that the holy River Ganges was flowing from his holy body. From time to time, his body will become hot. On some days, he will only chant 'gopi', 'gopi', 'gopi' and get outraged if anyone took the name of Krishna. On some other days, he will only utter 'gokul. 'gokul', 'gokul' or 'vrindavan', 'vrindavan', 'vrindavan' repeatedly. This *madhura bhava* represented pure love and compassion without any desire for physical sensory gratification. This was exactly what Sri Krishna used to have during his sport (*leela*) with the gopis and Sri Radhika. In excitement, his semen will move upwards, against gravity, towards the *sahasrara chakra* on top of the head instead of moving downwards as is normal. He would become *urdhareta* like Lord Shiva. Both were Supreme Gods after all.

The pull of the *dark matter* was much stronger than the pull of gravity. Sometimes, the moment he had entered into the Puri temple, if the place was relatively less crowded, he will run straight towards Lord Jagannath to hug him closely in order to earn the love-compassion-trust-and-bonding molecule *Oxytocin,* and lose his consciousness the urge was so strong. He will not get back to his senses for quite a long time – sometimes, three to four days.

The influence of the *madhura bhava* was so strong that while strolling on the Puri seabeach, he would hallucinate as if he was in Vrindavan; and start looking for Sri Krishna in the nearby bushes and greeneries. Swami Vivekananda had said: "He discovered Vrindavana by the power of insight he had acquired through devotion". (References 13–18)

Sri Chaitanya and Jagai-Madhai

Sri Chaitanya Mahaprabhu had engaged Thakur Sri Haridas and Sri Nityananda Prabhu to spread and promote the name of Sri Krishna in every home of Nabadwip. Once, Nityananda Prabhu (incarnation of Sri Krishna's elder brother Balaram) had spent the whole day promoting door-to-door the name of Krishna and was returning to Mahaprabhu's house, suddenly he met two young brahmins by the name of Jagai and Madhai. Both of them were branded sinners. One could not think of any heinous act that these two had not committed. Since they used to be in the company of drunkards all the time, they didn't have the opportunity to know anything much about the Vaishnavas. In any case, they were not religious or spiritual in the least. The moment they found Sri Nityananda Prabhu, Madhai threw a broken earthen pot towards him. It had hit Nityananda so hard that he had an injury in his forehead and started bleeding profusely. As soon as Sri Chaitanya heard about this incident, he arrived at the site with a few of his devotees. He was outraged finding the injury of Nityananda. However, instead of complaining against them, Nityananda said: "Jagai has saved me. Please forgive him". Mahaprabhu was pleased with Jagai. This brought about some change in Madhai's attitude also; and he was pardoned by Sri Krishna Chaitanya.

Jagai and Madhai both were most regretful and they promised not to commit any sin any longer; instead, they would devote their time and spend their time entirely by chanting the name of *Hari*. Finding these two branded sinners transformed, Mahaprabhu and his devotees were all very happy.

> "The Master says these two are no longer drunkards
> Instead, right from today they are committed to serve me.
> All of you share your grace and goodwill with them
> That in life after life they must not unfollow me.
> Whenever and whatever they might have instances of any sin
> Let them be forgiven with your kind gesture.
>
> As Jagai Madhai heard the Master's words
> They fell at the feet of everyone present.

All the great divine souls showered blessings on them
Jagai Madhai were acquitted of all their misdeeds.

The Master now says......get up you two Jagai Madhai
I am not worried any more as you have promised to serve me.
I have taken the misdeeds and sins of both of you into me
Nobody will regard you as sinners any more
It does not happen to anyone ever
You must know that you have earned the grace of Nityananda."

(Adapted from Sri Sri Nityananda Charitamrita, Adi Khanda Translated from Bengali into English by author)

In the above piece, the following things are noteworthy about the character of Sri Chaitanya Mahaprabhu:

1. He was an ocean of mercy and kindness. With him, there was always an opportunity for getting forgiven because he thought people commit a sin because of lack of true knowledge (*avidya*).
2. He expected *'dasya bhava'* from Jagai Madhai, which represents a spirit of total servitude. And,
3. He said that he had taken all the misdeeds and sins of both Jagai and Madhai into him. This, in terms of *Cosmology* and *Astrophysics*, is the *Black Hole* behaviour whereby the black hole sucks everything that comes in front of its siphoning funnel.

True Devotion: The 'White Hole' Analogy

Everyone is aware about the total devotion that sage Narada had for Bhagawan Sri Krishna. He used to think that there was no one who was superior to him in devotion. Sri Krishna faked illness as he wanted to shatter his vanity and ego. Being very much concerned, Narada asked: "My Lord what should I do to cure your illness and give you relief?" Sri Krishna told him that he will be cured only if he was offered the dust of the feet of authentic devotees. He sent Narada to all his wives but they were all most embarrassed at the thought of offering the dust of their feet to the Bhagawan. Narada was most disappointed. However, he wanted to take a last chance. He went to Vrindavan and asked the

Gopis. When the Gopis were told about the purpose, they readily agreed. Their only concern was how they could help in giving quick relief to Sri Krishna. Narada was overwhelmed to note the devotion of the Gopis and was convinced that they were certainly a step superior than him.

I find a similarity between true, authentic, unconditional devotion which represents 'Only Giving' and the 'White Hole' which spits out without sucking anything. Although 'White Hole' is still very much of a hypothetical concept, still I am tempted to use it as a most appropriate analogy for 'Unconditional Devotion'.

Let me share with you another example from Sri Chaitanya's life. The incident happened when Mahaprabhu was in Puri. One day, he was tired after his *kirtan* accompanied with dance. So, he had his *prasad* and laid down his body, near the doorway, for some rest. His devotee Gobinda just arrived at that time. However, since Sri Chaitanya had blocked the doorway, so Gobinda could not enter by crossing his Guru. He requested Chaitanya to turn a little on one side so that he could somehow manage to pass, but Chaitanya said he was too tired to move his body even an inch. Gobinda had a thought wave. He had a scarf (*chadar*) to be worn on top of his *kurta*. He took it and spread it over his Guru's body and crossed over to the other side. And, then instead of going inside to take his *prasad*, he sat there and started massaging his Guru's legs and feet. Sri Chaitanya fell asleep for a little while and when he woke up after some time, finding Gobinda massaging his body, he asked him why he had not gone to take his *prasad*. Gobinda said most humbly: "My Lord! I am massaging your feet and you are feeling so good that you fell asleep. How can I deprive you from feeling good and happy and run to have my *prasad*? I thought it would be too selfish, so I continued to give foot massage to you". This is the 'White Hole' concept – 'giving entirely' without 'taking anything to satisfy a self-interest'.

There is another very interesting and unique case I am sharing with you from Bhagawan Sri Krishna Chaitanya's life. This is about his Muslim devotee-companion who used to join him always in his *hari sankirtan*. His name was Thakur Sri Haridas. Although he was born in a Muslim family, he had a natural inclination for *harinam* since his childhood. Fouzdar Chand Kazi, the Muslim ruler of Nawadip, had complained to the Nawab about Haridas that he used to participate regularly in the *hari sankirtan* of the Hindus. At the Nawab's order, his security guards put Haridas behind the bars; but, even while in the prison, he used to chant the name of *hari* and sing *harinam* and would give good advice to his fellow prisoners. When the angry Nawab asked him, why being a Muslim, he was following some Hindu rituals, prompt came Haridas's reply:

> "Please lend your ears! Everyone has the same God
> It's only a difference in name between the Hindus and the Muslims
> In the Quran and the Puranas, the message is the same."

(Sri Chaitanya Bhagavad 16/76–77)

Despite the Nawab's repeated threats, Thakur Haridas had remained unperturbed and said:

> "Even if I am cut into several pieces
> I'll not give up chanting the name of *Lord Hari*"

(Sri Chaitanya Bhagavad 16/94)

The Nawab's guards were totally surprised when, even after Haridas was beaten by a cane twenty two times, he did not give up his *kirtan*. On the contrary, he prayed to Lord Krishna:

> "Oh, Lord Krishna! Please have mercy on these people
> Please forgive all their misdeeds and sins!"

I find here Thakur Sri Haridas was praying to and requesting Bhagawan Sri Krishna to act like a 'Black Hole' and suck all the misdeeds and sins of the Nawab and his guards instead of complaining against them and requesting Him to punish them.

Thakur Haridas had wished that Mahaprabhu Sri Chaitanya Dev must remain by the side of his deathbed. Mahaprabhu had kept his request. Haridas kept Sri Chaitanya's both feet on his chest and went into *mahasamadhi* most peacefully. Sri Chaitanya said most regretfully:

"Oh, Lord Krishna! You had given me a wonderful companion
But, now that you've taken him away from me,
I've nothing to say!"

(Sri Chaitanya Bhagavad 11/94)

A Muslim tailor was too much impressed to witness Sri Chaitanya's dance. Bhagawan Mahaprabhu also raised himself above religious barriers and showed the tailor his real form. The tailor was so overwhelmed with joy that he himself started dancing.

There was a young Suklambar Brahmachari who used to live in Nabadwip. He used to chant the name of Lord Krishna all the time. He used to go from house to house with his begging bowl to earn his livelihood. Local people used to downgrade him and call him a beggar. One day Sri Chaitanya called him and expressed his wish to eat food cooked by him. Beggar Suklambar was scared at Mahaprabhu wanting to eat food cooked by him. He said: "Master! I am a poor beggar and you are like God to us. Please don't ridicule me by wanting to have food cooked by me."

Sri Chaitanya remarked: "I'm not ridiculing you for a moment. You are such a great devotee of Lord Krishna. I am too serious about eating food cooked by your hand. Please go and prepare something for me." The other devotees present there counselled Suklambar that Sri Chaitanya was an ocean of kindness. He loved everyone. So, they pleaded him to go and prepare something.

Suklambar cooked something with lot of love and care while chanting the name of Lord Krishna. Mahaprabhu Sri Chaitanya went to Suklambar's house with Sri Nityananda and others, ate the food cooked by Suklambar after offering some to Sri Krishna and sharing portions with his companions, praising most profusely the quality and taste of the preparations. Suklambar, the so-called beggar was more than just happy and pleased.

Bhagawan Sri Krishna Chaitanya used to say: "I am neither a brahmin; nor am I a kshatriya king, or a vaishya or sudra. Neither am I a *brahmachari* or a householder, a retiree or a *sannyasi*, I am just a servant of the all-powerful Sri Krishna. That is what I am".

Sri Chaitanya was far away from the level of consciousness that discriminates one religion or one caste from another, or a poor man from a rich man. Such souls have no discriminatory *Error Neurons* in their brain.

Following is a verse which depicts Bhagawan Sri Krishna Chaitanya as a *black hole* sucking all the sins and misdeeds of sinners and miscreants:

> "Even low-born, sinful souls entrapped in Kali's Age,
> Suffering unnumbered pains that no one can assuage,
> Are instantly delivered when You kindly seek them out
> And flood them with Your splendid mercy, making bhakti sprout.
> And so with heart rejoicing at Your mercy's endless store,
> I take full shelter of Your lotus feet and then implore
> O Lord Chaitanya! Sri Mukunda! Sachi's precious jewel,
> Please shower your compassion on the wretched, stubborn fool."

—H.G. Dravida Dasa
(References 19–22)

Sri Chaitanya's *White Hole* Behaviour

Gobinda Chandra Ghosh was one who had set up the famous 'Gopinath' idol of Agradwip.

One day, when Mahaprabhu Sri Chaitanya, along with a few of his devotees, was taking bath in the Holy River Ganges, Gobinda arrived there. He was most impressed to see the luminous face of the young ascetic. He fell at the feet of Gouranga and said, with tears in his eyes: 'Oh, My Lord! I do not want to lead a householder's life. I am not after wealth, name or fame. I only want to serve your lotus feet". Listening to him, Gouranga Dev started talking to him about the advantages of a householder's life. Gobinda was unperturbed and said: "Money, prosperity and status cannot allure me any longer. Please give me a place at your feet." Mahaprabhu took the man to be a real devotee, gave him a good hug and told him: "You can stay with me if you're really free from any desire and demand." Gobinda agreed readily.

Once he took *sannyas*, Mahaprabhu was residing at Neelachal at the instance of his mother's order. It is customary for *sannyasis* to visit their birthplace once after leaving the householder's life. On the day of *Vijaya Dasami*, Mahaprabhu and all his devotees based at Neelachal, barring Gadadhar, left for Gour to visit his mother Sachi Devi and also the Holy River Ganges.

After they spent a few days at Nabadwip, they bade farewell to Sachi Mata and proceeded towards Vrindavan. Many devotees were accompanying him and, amongst them, Gobinda Ghosh was also there. As *sannyasis*, they had no belongings with them. While singing and dancing with *kirtan* whichever village they would reach on the way, the villagers had to extend the hospitality.

When they reached Agradwip, after having something to eat from whatever they had got by begging, Mahaprabhu extended his hand for some *mukhsuddhi*. Gobinda ran to a villager's home and brought some 'myrobalan' (*hurituki*). One piece he gave to Sri Gouranga and the other piece he saved by tying a knot in his dhoti.

On the next day, after a meal Mahaprabhu said: "It seems, today, I've to go without any *mukhsuddhi*." The devotees present were all quiet. Suddenly, Gobinda said: "My Lord! I still have a piece of 'myrobalan' with me. If you permit me, I will offer it for your *seba*."

Chaitanya Dev said, smilingly: "Gobinda, I'm accepting your offer gladly. But from today, you leave my company." (It was a *white hole* behaviour on the part of Sri Chaitanya that he rejected Gobinda outright.)

Gobinda was, as if, thunder struck – as he had never expected such a reaction from Mahaprabhu. He broke into tears and asked: "What wrong have I done that you have been so strict with me?"

Chaitanya Dev replied, most affectionately: "Gobinda! You're a good devotee and quite eligible for worshipping Lord Hari. But you have not been able to observe total freedom from desires – as, I find, you still have the instinct for saving. That is why I am telling you to return – worship Lord Hari – which will lead you to liberation."

"I don't want anything as I have given up everything. I am not going to return to householder's life." On hearing this from Gobinda, Mahaprabhu embraced him and said: "It is absolutely right that you have given up everything, but you still have a tendency to acquire things. Today, you have saved the piece of 'myrobalan'; tomorrow, you might be tempted to save something else. This propensity itself is dangerous. You please go back home."

Gobinda started crying and rolling on the ground. Mahaprabhu was adamant: "Gobinda! You'll not be able to go to Vrindavan. Instead, it is better that you stay in Agradwip itself. Please don't feel bad – there are quite a few things I want to be done by you here. And, someday, if some miracle happens to you, you'll see and meet me again. You stay here. I will return soon. Don't worry. I will not leave you. If you get something miraculously, please preserve it with care. Your wishes will be fulfilled."

This is a very good example of Bhagawan Sri Chaitanya's *white hole* behaviour.

Sri Chaitanya's Sudden Turn Towards Krishna Consciousness

Bhagawan Sri Krishna Chaitanya lived for forty-eight years. During the first half of his life – the first twenty-four years, his childhood and boyhood were full of naughtiness and childish misdeeds for earning the cheap and easily available neuro-transmitter *'Dopamine'* (*'D'*). During his early youth also, he had a big 'ego' and used to criticise and ridicule all his friends and others of the same age group to earn cheap pleasure (*'Dopamine'* income again). He wanted to prove that he was the best amongst them. Often, he would challenge them about their knowledge of Sanskrit grammar. He used to reject people outright instead of looking at their strengths and 'plus points'. His behaviour was typical of a *white hole*, which ejects and spits everything instead of allowing anything to enter inside. Then there was a sudden 360 degree turn towards total positivity as he came in very close contact with Iswar Puri who was a disciple of the well-known *Vaishnava* sadhak Madhavendra Puri. Iswar Puri was much impressed with Nimai's handsome looks, tall stature and golden complexion. To my mind, it was possible as Iswar Puri was a 'devoted' devotee of the *Dark God* Sri Krishna who, because of his pure unstinted devotion, had developed a *black hole* nature – ready to suck anyone who had a dormant potential to develop 'Krishna Consciousness'. Nimai's meeting with Iswar Puri was a most effective 'trigger' for his sudden most unexpected transformation which made him quit all other pursuits like teaching Sanskrit grammar. Inside Nimai's brain's *Pituitary Glands* (*PiG*), the floodgates of the trust molecule *'Oxytocin'* (*'O'*) suddenly got opened and a deep bonding developed between him and Sri Krishna devotee Iswar Puri.

Sri Krishna Chaitanya's Role Model: Madhavendra Puri

The Vaishnava movement that began in the 16th century under the influence of Bhagawan Sri Krishna Chaitanya Mahaprabhu had its initiation even earlier. One Vaishnava practitioner who had paved the path which was later followed by Sri Chaitanya was Madhavendra Puri. Madhavendra was a monk from Bengal. Overwhelmed by the devotional love of Lord Krishna, he moved over to Vrindavandham and spent many years meditating on the Dark God in a small hut at the bank of the Holy River Yamuna. His desire to get close to Lord Krishna was so strong that he never had any time to beg and cook whatever he got from his begging rounds. He ate only the food offered to him by those who came to his hut to take his blessings. Most of the days, he went without consuming anything. Naturally, his health deteriorated and he became very weak. Since he was always full of the thoughts of Lord Krishna, the Dark God was attuned to his thoughts and felt for his dedicated devotee. It is said that Sri Krishna took the form of a cowherd boy and brought milk for him and made sure that he drank it.

Once the Bhagwan had appeared before Madhavendra in his dream. He informed him that one idol of him in his *gopal* form is hidden under ground as the brahmin priest who used to worship him had put it there so that the Muslim invaders could not destroy it. The Lord told Madhavendra the place where it was hidden and instructed him to dig it out and put it in a proper place so that it could be regularly worshipped. Madhavendra located the place, took out the idol from underground and set it up in a proper place for worship. When people got to know about it, many started pouring in to make their offerings. The place became sacred like a religious shrine.

Madhavendra Puri had nothing but Krishna thoughts in his mind. Nothing else could find a place there. The whole night, he wouldn't sleep – instead he will think about the Dark God. He used to find him inside the dark monsoon clouds. He used to hear his voice in the sound of thunder. He used to find his aura in the luminosity of the lightning. He used to behave like a mad man having been drunk with the liquor of *Krishna Prem* (the love for Lord Krishna). Drunkards behave normally once the hangover is gone; but in the case of Madhavendra who was drunk with the wine of love for Lord Krishna, his hangover would persist permanently. With that state of mind, Madhavendra started for Puri from Vrindavan on foot to collect some special offerings.

Once, when he was in the Kripavarta Valley in South India, Sri Chaitanya's friend Nityananda was also present there on some special mission. Nityananda found Madhavendra in deep trance (*bhav-samadhi*), radiating bright *aura* from his whole body. He fell at his feet, held them in his hand and placed those on his chest with a feeling of deep devotion. With tears in his eyes, he said: "I feel so blessed today; my birth has been worthwhile."

Amongst Madhavendra's Bengali disciples, two most prominent ones were: Keshava Bharati and Ishwar Puri. Both of them had served as *Gurus* to Sri Krishna Chaitanya. Chaitanya Dev had never seen or met Madhavendra. But, whenever he used to chant some *slokas* composed by him, he used to get ecstatic. He used to get body tremor and would perspire, become pale with remorse – as if late Madhavendra Puri's soul would enter into him and would become inseparable. (References 23–28)

The Essence of Bhagawan Sri Krishna Chaitanya's Spirituality and Bhakti Yoga

Some scholars say that in Bhagawan Sri Krishna Chaitanya's Spirituality and Bhakti Yoga, there is a shadow of Sufi-ism, especially how he had recommended the process to be followed and practiced singing *kirtans* and dancing following the rhythm. One can, most strikingly, note a difference in Chaitanya's practices – which represent spontaneous devotion (*'bhakti'*) flavoured by *'Pure Love'* (*'Prem'*) contrary to ritualistic devotion aiming at 'liberation' by logical understanding.

I am tempted to share a stanza from a Vaishnava masterpiece:

> "The urge for purely personal sensory gratification is
> 'carnal desire' (*'kam'* in Sanskrit)
> And your wish to have Lord Krishna as your own kin is
> 'spiritual desire' (*prem*' in Sanskrit)!
> 'Carnal desire' is absolutely selfish related to the 'I'
> 'Spiritual desire' is most powerful as your wish is
> to unite with Lord Krishna,
> the preserver of the universe!!'

(English adaptation from Chaitanya Charitamrita) (References 29 & 30)

Sri Krishna Chaitanya Mahaprabhu & His Krishna Consciousness

Chaitanya Mahaprabhu, although he was a golden-skinned person, his 'Krishna Consciousness' had made his *Soul* overflowing with *Dark Energy*, derived from the Dark God Krishna. So, can you realise why his *'Hare Krishna' sankirtan-based* movement caught up so fast? It was because he was distributing the most powerful *Dark Energy* absolutely, 'free for all'.

His process for reaching God was very simple, unlike the ways followed by Pundits and Scholars reciting from the scriptures and chanting *stutis*. A devotee would just have to chant *Hare Krishna* and dance, sometimes whirling in planetary motion like a Sufi *dervish*. Such circular dancing is called *hallish* in Sanskrit. The devotional process did not require any special knowledge, training or even literacy and could be followed by anyone from any religion, caste, creed or any level of the society.

In Srimad Bhagavad Gita, many kinds of 'sacrifices' (*'yajna'*) have been included, but there is no mention of any 'sacrifice' using the act of singing and dancing in praise (which is *'sankirtan'*). Mahaprabhu had mentioned to his associates:

> "*Sankirtan* of God's name is the most effective way of worshipping Him. It is a 'sacrifice' (because you are surrendering your 'ego' – that is why it is a 'sacrifice') that leads you to the feet of Lord Krishna. It dispels all useless vibes and fills you with *pure love* for Krishna."

"For long he sang and danced
influenced by pure love
Many came to watch him
and all people around said "Hari! Hari!"
In their midst, Gourhari danced on
in a trance-like state."

(Sri Chaitanya Charitamrita) (Reference 31)

Dark Energy Has Healing Power

In a Bengali novel on the reincarnation of Bhagawan Sri Krishna Chaitanya, the incarnate Gora had an accidental cut in his foot which was attended by a local doctor. The next day, the doctor and his wife came to see Gora. The doctor's wife was ecstatic when she said that the doctor had a swelling in his throat which he was most reluctant to have removed through surgery. Most miraculously, the swelling had totally disappeared after he had touched Gora's foot on the previous day while dressing the wound. Gora had been brimming with devotion for the dark god Krishna; so, apparently, it was the dark energy which had worked on the swelling on the doctor's throat and made it subside. (References 32 & 33)

Effect of Dark Energy Deprivation

At times, when Mahaprabhu (in his *Radha* Bhava) used to suffer from acute anxiety due to separation from Sri Krishna (equivalent to *dark energy deprivation*), recitation or chanting from the verses of Joydeb,

Vidyapati and Chandidas used to reduce his restlessness – so effective were the poetic works of those three classical poets.

Srila Raghunath Das Goswami, regular companion of Sri Chaitanya Mahaprabhu during the last phase of his life, writes in his literary work *Chaitanya Staba Kalpataru* (2nd Sloka):

> "One day, in *Gambhira,* as the Puri house of Kashi Mishra was known, suffering from the anxiety of separation from Bhagawan Sri Krishna, Sri Chaitanya was found to have lost his lustrous aura, all the joints of his long limbs became loose resulting in his extremities becoming still longer. With that decrepit physical condition, he was rolling on the floor of the room and sobbing in great grief."

Did it happen when Sri Chaitanya had the *Sri Radhika Soul* dominant in his personality – longing deeply for her beloved *Dark God Krishna*? A most pertinent question arises in my mind.

The same incident had also been described by Krishnadas Kaviraj in his Chaitanya literature although there was a little difference. However, what I want to highlight is that Sri Chaitanya's whole spiritual existence used to thrive on the *dark energy* that he used to derive from the Dark God Krishna; and, whenever he used to be deprived of that energy due to some reason (which was variable), he used to suffer physically as had been described in *Chaitanya Staba Kalpataru.*

Krishnadas Kaviraja's version is as follows:

> "From the evening time itself, Chaitanya was almost unconscious in a 'trance-like' state. Ramananda brought him back to senses, only partially, by midnight by reciting different *slokas* and singing 'Krishna Leela' songs to him. Laying him in that state on bed, Ramananda retired in his own room. Swarup and Govinda slept near the front door of *Gambhira.* Later, sometime during late night, when there was no sound from inside the room where Chaitanya was asleep, Swarup opened the door to find, to his utter surprise, that Chaitanya was missing. He was not to be found anywhere in the premises. All the three doors connecting the house to the outside ground were shut. Most anxious associates of Chaitanya started

searching for him everywhere and ultimately found his unconscious body lying on the north side of the main entrance to the Jagannath temple. All the joints in his arms, hands, legs and feet were found to be limp and loose increasing the lengths of his already long extremities. Froth was coming out of his mouth and his eyes had rotated to some extent." (References 34 & 35)

Sri Chaitanya – A Spiritual Change-maker

Right after his emergence as a *spiritual change-maker*, Sri Chaitanya could feel, very strongly, the need for the arousal of a real emotional vibration in hearts of the masses, for making the dry soil wet for cultivation of love-filled devotion. He realised that was more important than scripture-based ritualistic worships, and festivals and ceremonies on a grand scale that was prevalent in the Hindu religious culture when he first appeared on the scene. He found there was a perceptible distance between the worshipped and the worshippers. His goal was to bridge this gap.

His emphasis was on establishing a very close relationship between God and the masses, based on pure, unconditional devotional love. And, in this respect, his main supporter and helper was Sri Nityananda Prabhu. He was convinced that the best way to come close to Lord Krishna was by loving Him as a kin, by becoming His most obedient servant (*Dasya Bhava*) or His most intimate friend (*Sakhya Bhava*), or by playing the most benevolent parent role (*Vatsalya Bhava*), or by playing the role of His lover (*Madhura Bhava*). Nevertheless, no other worshipping strategies would, he strongly believed, would bring you close to the Supreme Lord than the 'best lover' role being that of Sri Radhika.

His devotees would witness the *persona* of both Krishna and Radha manifested in his body, postures, gestures, and gait. He disbanded all distinctions of caste, creed and financial status and propagated that anyone would be considered a 'great soul' if he had his heart filled with unconditional love and devotion for Hari and that even people from the highest strata of the society would be regarded as 'low' if they had no love-filled devotion for the *Dark God.*

Bengal and Orissa were fertile lands. The inhabitants did not have to migrate to other distant places to find food. This attracted Muslims and Buddhists and, later, Christians to convert confused Hindus into their religious faiths. So, the priority for the local people was not to take care, in modern biological terms, their *Second Brain* (the 'gut' – the 'Enteric Nervous System') but their *Third Brain* (the 'heart' and the 'Cardio-respiratory Nervous System'). This basic realisation led Chaitanya Dev to propagate and promote a free-for-all religious practice of *Nam Sankirtan*, which happens to be a very effective strategy for management of the brain's *'Default Mode Network'* (*'DMN'*) which is not only most disturbing but it also drain's out the most precious neural energy when there is no task in hand. (References 36 & 37)

Sri Chaitanya Dev: Bi-Gender Persona in a Male Body

Within a few days of Gouranga's return from Gaya, when he embarked upon his *Nabadwip-Leela*, his admirers and associates could witness that, at times, he was in the *nari bhava* of the *Gopis* (including that of *Sri Radhika*, and the *naro/veera bhava* of *Krishna*. But it is doubtful whether that facet of the *avatar* was clearly understood by them or it was masked by what they had thought as the main purpose of his existence: to bring about a big change in the dry way the Hindu religion was practised in those days, laying the whole thrust on rituals and observing strict caste distinction in the process. Once Sri Chaitanya Dev had set the ball of the *nam sankirtan* rolling, all Hindus from all castes and creeds joined in the movement and it took a massive shape.

However, once Chaitanya Dev shifted to Neelachal, the last twelve years of his life, his close companions could see him totally immersed in the devotion of the *Dark God*. The *nari bhava* in his persona had taken the front seat, so strong was his desire to get united with *Krishna*. He was totally *'Krishna Conscious'*. It had never happened during his *Nabadwip Leela*.

In English language, the two genders – male and female, are separate from each other. In Bengali, which was Chaitanya's vernacular, there is no such separation. It is thus implied that the same person – whether male or female, have both the 'personas' in the *Soul* and depending upon the circumstances, one of those comes to the surface and gets expressed or manifested. It was so in Chaitanya's case, vividly visible. So, it was in the case of *avatar* Sri Sri Ramakrishna. Is it because both these *avatars* were madly attracted towards *dark energy* present in Krishna and Kali.

I find an interesting analogy when we look at the human brain. It is often thought that each half or side of our brain is associated with a specific gender: for a right-handed person, the left corresponding with masculinity and the right with femininity. Language – grammar, vocabulary and literal meanings, and arithmetical calculations are typically lateralized to the left hemisphere whereas social interactions, demonstrating deep emotions (such as 'separation anxiety'), imagination, visualisation, creativity and mathematical information (geometry, algebra, trigonometry, and differential equations) are all provided by the right hemisphere. The left hemisphere tends to reduce complex matters such as ethics to rules and measures and the right hemisphere is disposed to holistic and metaphorical inputs. The left brain is thus responsible for functions like logic, analysis, reasoning, worldly pragmatism, number crunching – which are typically masculine whereas the right brain is the source of creativity, intuition, spirituality, artistry and big-picture thinking. The left brain's functions can be measured, the right brain functions cannot be. Just like, the males can be evaluated and their behaviours can be anticipated and predicted; whereas females cannot be so readily.

As a human scientist specialising in the human brain, I find Bhagawan Sri Krishna Chaitanya's case is a strikingly interesting one where in a male body he had a female soul (of the *Maha Gopi Sri Radhika*) crazy about union with the most attractive male God *Sri Krishna.* (References 38 & 39)

References

[1] Subhajit Ghosh, "The Story of Reincarnation: Sri Krishna and Sri Radhika", *LinkedIn*, 6th September 2023.

[2] Aranyakanda, "Vaishnavaganza: Chaitanya Mahaprabhu/Radha Krishna", *Rathangapani*, 14th April, 2013.

[3] "Shri Chaitanya Mahaprabhu: Embodiment of Sri Radha's Love" – *Radhanath Swami Yatras.*

[4] "Who is greater!" Video on YouTube by Gourangadas

[5] "Oxytocin" – *Wikipedia.*

[6] Paul J. Zak, *The Moral Molecule: How Trust Works*, New York: Plume (Penguin Group), 2013.

[7] "Ramananda Ray" – *Wikipedia.*

[8] Shyama Prasad Chattaraj, *Itihaser Path Dhore Vaishnav Dharma O Vaishnav Sahitya*, (In Bengali), Kolkata: Sahityasree, 2021, pp. 30–31, pp 36–37, pp. 46–47, p. 85.

[9] Girijashankar Roychaudhuri, *Sri Chaitanyadev O Tahar Parshadgan* (In Bengali), Calcutta: University of Calcutta, 1957, p. 4.

[10] "Gita Govinda" – *Wikipedia.*

[11] Nrisingha Prasad Bhaduri, *Chaitanyadev*, (In Bengali) Kolkata: Deep Prakashan, 6th Deep Impression, 2023, pp. 46–51.

[12] "Tota Gopinath Temple" – *Tirtha Yatra.*

[13] "Krishna Store".

[14] "Oxytocin" – *Wikipedia.*

[15] "Testosterone" – *Wikipedia.*

[16] Sumon Bhattacharya, *Dui Avatar: Sri Chaitanya O Sri Ramakrishna*, (In Bengali), Kolkata: Girija Library, 2020, pp. 57–58, p. 59, pp. 61–63, pp. 71–72, pp. 77–82, pp. 93–95.

[17] Mihalyi Csikszentmihalyi, *Flow: The Psychology of Optimal Experience*, 2002, London: Rider (Random House Group).

[18] VivekVani, "Swami Vivekananda's Quotes On Chaitanya Mahaprabhu", *VivekVani*, 27th August 2017.

[19] "Black Hole" – *Wikipedia.*

[20] "White Hole" – *Wikipedia.*

[21] "Error Neurons" *Cedars-Sinai*, 6th August 2019.

[22] "Why Did Lord Krishna Appear as Lord Chaitanya in the Present Age, Kali-yuga?" ISKCON San Diego Live TV, Class by HG Dravida Dasa.

[23] Nrisingha Prasad Bhaduri, *Chaitanyadev*, (In Bengali) Kolkata: Deep Prakashan, Sixth Deep Impression, pp. 98–100.

[24] "What If a Black Hole and a White Hole Collided?" Video Presentation on YouTube, IF – What If Channel.

[25] "What Happens When A White Hole And A Black Hole Collide?" Video Presentation on You Tube, Space Academy Channel.

[26] Krishnadasa Kaviraja, *Chaitanya Charitamrita*, (In Bengali) Adi 9, pp. 10–11.

[27] "Black Holes Target Space Objects", WION Podcast, Video Presentation on You Tube.

[28] Shyama Prasad Chattaraj, *Itihaser Path Dhore Vaishnav Dharma O Vaishnav Sahitya* (In Bengali), Kolkata: Sahityasree, 2021, pp. 42–45.

[29] Mohan Kali Biswas, *Gauriya Baishnav Dharmer Abakkhyaer Karon* (In Bengali), Kolkata: Dey's Publishing, 2017, pp. 15–17.

[30] Krishnadasa Kaviraja , *Chaitanya Charitamrita* (In Bengali with a number of Sanskrit verses), originally 1557

[31] Mohan Kali Biswas, *Gaudiya Baishnav Dharmer Abakkhayer Karon* (In Bengali), Kolkata: Dey's Publishing, 2017, pp. 60 – 65.

[32] Rupak Saha, *Khsama Karo He Prabhu* (In Bengali), Kolkata: Deep Prakashan, 10th Impression, 2023, p. 470

[33] Koijam Manihar Singh and Kangujam Priyokumar Singh, "Whether dark energy can contribute to the treatment and healing of diseases", *Modern Physics Letters A*, 2019, Vol. 34, No. 32, 1950260.

[34] Jibendu Ray, *Gaudiya Baishnab Darshan Pad O Padakar*, (In Bengali) Kolkata: Sahityasree, New Reconstructed Edition 2023.

[35] Tuhin Mukhopadhyay, *Chaitanyer Sesh Prahar* (In Bengali), Kolkata: Patralekha, 7th Impression, 2023, pp. 91–93.

[36] Mohan Kali Biswas, *Gaudiya Baishnav Dharmer Abakkhayer Karon* (In Bengali), Kolkata: Dey's Publishing, 2017, pp. 89 – 92.

[37] Randy L. Buckner, "The brain's default network: origins and implications for the study of psychosis", *Dialogues in Clinical Neuroscience*, Vol. 15, No/Issue 3, September 2013, pp. 351–358/National Library of Medicine.

[38] "Lateralization of the Human Brain" – *Wikipedia.*

[39] Douglas Todd, "Beyond the 'left' and 'right' brain – the science of spirituality and art. *Vancouver Sun*, 16th November 2013.

[*Note:* Please watch the concluding scene of the Hindi Movie *Shri Chaitanya Mahaprabhu*, starring Nitish Bharadwaj, Madhu and Saheb Chatterjee on You Tube 'Hindi Movies' Channel where Mahaprabhu is being sucked into the Dark God Lord Jagannath's body – a *black hole* phenomenon.]

CHAPTER 4

Sri Sri Ramakrishna

Shyama, Not An Ordinary Girl

"Oh, My Mind! You don't know
the main reason
Why Shyama is not an ordinary girl!!

At times, she takes the male form
by changing her looks akin to
the deep and dark blue clouds!!

Oh, My Mind! You don't know
the main reason
Shyama is not an ordinary girl!!

At times, she has matted hair
At other times, she has a pony tail
on which she puts a peacock feather
In that outfit, she goes to the land
where Sri Krishna was to play as a kid
(to the village named *Braja*, near *Mathura*)
and plays the flute
The sweet melody mesmerises the villagers there!!

Oh, My mind! You don't know
the main reason
Why Shyama is not just an ordinary girl!!

She enters and inhabits in the mind
of people in exactly the way
each of her devotees want her to be!!

She arises, appears and remains as a lotus girl
in the heart-pond of Kamalakanta!!

Oh! My mind! You don't know
the main reason
Why Shyama is just not an ordinary girl
At times, she takes the male form
by changing her looks akin to
the deep and dark blue clouds!!
Oh! My Mind! You don't know
the main reason
Why Shyama is not an ordinary girl!!

[The original song was composed by Sadhak Kamalakanta (Bhattacharya) (1769–1821) who was a Bengali *shakta* poet and yogi of India of the late 18th century. The English translation is mine.]

In this poem, the poet tries to establish that the dark Goddess Kali (she is also known as *Shyama* by another name) and the dark God Sri Krishna are no different from each other – they are the same *dark energy* in two different forms; that's all! What a fantastic idea – it tallies very well with what I am trying to establish that these dark goddesses and gods of Hinduism all represent the *dark matter* in their deity forms having *potential dark energy* stored in the images. As and when they become active, the *potential energy* becomes *kinetic* and provides the power for all their respective scheduled actions. That is why the songwriter says that 'Shyama is not just an ordinary girl'. Spiritually highly advanced souls can change their forms according to the circumstances in which they are placed. They have a high degree of *situational flexibility* which is an excellent example of the human brain's *plasticity* – one of my favourite topics as a Brain Scholar and Neuro-scientist. It relates to the domain of *Neuro-management* that I've created. [Refer to around 50 videos on 'Neuro-management Tips' by me posted on YouTube.]

Young Gadadhar (Sri Sri Ramakrishna's formal name), as a pre-teen boy had his very first ecstatic experience of *samadhi* ('God Consciousness') when he was roaming around in a paddy field, munching puffed rice in a small basket. It was monsoon season, and suddenly he found a flock of snow-white cranes flying across the overcast black sky. The dark colour 'black' providing the background for the flying white cranes. Gadadhar was a fair-skinned boy and his spiritual mother Goddess

Kali was black. Both were striking contrasts. That was Gadadhar's very first spiritual experience as he lost consciousness, fell down on the ground with the puffed rice spread all over the marshy paddy field. That day was the beginning of his divine ecstatic experiences (*brahma jnan*) which would last throughout his life.

Later on, the experienced *Avatar* used to compare *samadhi* with going into 'black water' (*kaala pani*). When you look into the ocean, the distant water looks *black* or *dark*. *Samadhi* is entering into *darkness* – your mind is absolutely vacant like a *black screen*. When you return from your *samadhi* the mind is lighted again with full consciousness. So, *nirvikalpa samadhi* is meeting with *darkness*. (Reference 1–5)

The Black Girl

"In the soles of the Black Girl's feet
the dance of light can be seen.
Having gazed upon the Mother's beauty,
Lord Shiva offered his chest,
to She in whose hand is both death and salvation.
In that Black Girl's dark embrace
She holds her children, the Sun and the Moon,
rocking them back and forth;
A mere sparkling fragment of the Mother's beauty
becalms our spirit on the great blue sky
That Crazy Girl with the wild hair,
shakes Her head and brings nightfall;
As She dances about the day dissipates
like a burning funeral pyre
this dear one's magic is without end
The ocean to Her is like a drop of water
She shines resplendent like a jewel
The universe cannot contain

Mother's transcendent beauty
and that is why my Mother is naked.

–Nazrul Islam

(The song, originally composed in Bengali, has been translated into English by William Clark; Reference: 'Kalo Meyer Payer Tolay': A Song by Nazrul Islam' and posted on kalibhakti.com on 15th March 2017)

The composer, Kazi Nazrul Islam (1899–1976), the national poet of Bangladesh, explored various creative and social territories throughout his prolific life. At heart, he was a pure humanist as otherwise why being a Muslim by birth he would write so devotedly about a Hindu goddess and, in his personal life, would marry a Hindu lady. He is mostly famous for composing nearly 4,000 songs and creating his own musical genre called *Nazrul Geeti.*

The first two lines of the song reminds me of the glittering stars and planets as well as galaxies in the vast womb of the *dark matter* of the universe. In the next line, we find the contrast between fairness and darkness just like the day-and-night rhythm of Mother Nature. Thereafter, the Goddess is being compared with the vast dark space which is where the Sun and the Moon are positioned to repeat their own cycles non-stop.

Goddess Kali is normally 'cold'. She becomes 'hot' and 'exceedingly hot' when she has to kill the 'asuras'. She became 'warm' with affection and love only when she was 'pulled' by the child-like *Avatar* Sri Sri Ramakrishna. For ordinary people like us, the *Paramatma* is the *Brahmanda* (*cosmos, Dark Matter*), and our individual soul (*jivatma*) has to provide the gravitational pull for the *Cosmic Energy (*that is, *Dark Energy*) to descend to get energized to perform tasks of a 'spiritual' nature.

'Dark Matter' Becomes Alive in Dream

Let me share an unbelievably interesting case study.

In 1847, a most prominent wealthy widow landlady Rani Rashmoni, from the British Province of Bengal, had the desire to set up a temple to worship the Divine Mother Goddess. She was preparing to go by boat from Calcutta to the sacred city of Varanasi in order to translate her wishful scheme into reality. The night before she had planned to leave, the Divine Mother appeared in her dream in the form of the Dark Goddess Kali, telling her that there was no need for her to go to Varanasi and that, instead, if she looked for, she would find a very special land to erect a temple to install Her statue on the banks of the Holy River Ganges and arrange for Her worship there. Why move so far away to Varanasi as Calcutta was most auspicious where the toes of the right foot of Devi Sati had fallen at Kalighat in the course of her husband Shiva's Rudra Tandava.

Search for a suitable land ended when a huge area resembling the hump of a tortoise ('*Kurma*' in Sanskrit) was found. What a spiritual connection!! One part of the land belonged to a European Christian while the other part was a Muslim burial ground; and, 20 acres of land was procured to build a Hindu religious shrine consisting of several temples, the main one being for the Dark Goddess Kali, and 12 other temples dedicated Lord Shiva, as well as a special one for the divine couple Sri Radha and Bhagawan Krishna. The representative colour of a cremation or a burial ground is *black*. What a coincidence! The temple for a *black* goddess was going to be built on a land which represented the *black* colour. May we thus take it that Rani Rasmoni also represented *black* colour? Caste-wise she was a *Jalia Kaibarta* – a community that comprised people of low ritual status, fishermen, fish and water both representing dark greyish colour.

Accordingly, an auspicious site was selected, the basalt stone image of the deity was ordered, and construction work got started.

The pious Rani had started observing strict religious chores and practices from the very day the sculptor had started working on the stone image. The image was ready but the construction of the temple and its adjoining buildings were going on rather at a slow pace. Lest the deity's image gets broken, it was put in an iron chest and locked up. Suddenly, one day Rani Ma got a feeling that the stone image of the Goddess was talking to her from inside the iron chest, as if she was alive: "For how long more you'll keep me locked up like this; I am getting suffocated. It is a most trying experience for me. Please take me out soon and set me up".

This particular case – does it not indicate that the basalt stone image (which is equivalent to 'dark matter') got energized (with the help of the dormant 'dark energy' stored in its atoms and molecules) and appeared to Rani Rasmoni in her dream? Some people say, when the iron chest was opened, those who were present could see drops of sweat on the deity's body, as if she was a living Goddess who had perspired having been locked up in an iron chest for quite some time.

(References 6 & 7)

Why a Land Shaped Like the Tortoise Hump is Considered Most Auspicious?

Lord Vishnu knew that if the demons (Asuras & Danavas, in Sanskrit) became immortal due to the boon received from some great sage, then they would overpower the Gods (Devas in Sanskrit) and also cause massive damage to the human race. Vishnu, out of the Trinity (Brahma-Vishnu-Maheswara), played the 'protector' role. Therefore, to save the human kind, from the demons, He took the Avatar form of a tortoise (Kurma, in Sanskrit) to be able to provide shelter to the humans under his huge hump. This was Vishnu's second avatarhood after the first one, centuries earlier, when he had taken the form of a fish (Matsya, in Sanskrit). As the supreme protector, Lord Vishnu had pledged that he would appear every time someone threatened the existence of humanity. He had taken the vow that he would take an avatar form on earth to restore Justice (Dharma, in Sanskrit) by uprooting lack of Justice (Adharma). For the uninitiated the Tri-Devas (Brahma-Vishnu-Maheswara) symbolised Dharma while the demons represented Adharma. (Reference 8)

The Living Goddess Kali of North Kolkata

We are all very much aware of Thakur Ramakrishna's sport (*leela*) with Goddess Kali – the *Jagattarini* of the Dakshineswar Kali temple. We have read how he used to talk to her, share *bhog* and *prasad* with her, climb on to her bed, try to sit on her lap; which, however, nobody else could see. Those present while he would worship could only experience how devotedly he used to perform being immersed in a totally different mood. His was at a very high level of *Bhakti Yoga,* combined with *Prem* – not just *bhakti* as a typical good priest will do. His was devotion mixed with pure, unconditional love and longing, which led to the *Oxytocin Effect. Oxytocin ('O')* is the neuro-transmitter representing unconditional love-affection-understanding-empathy-and-trust. Secreted from the *Pituitary Glands ('PiG')* glands of our brain, it serves as the bonding molecule to put the relationship between two persons on a very tight, solid foundation. (Reference 9)

Recently, I came across the news of a living Goddess Kali in North Kolkata's Sukea Street Shyamsundari temple. Goddess Kali is worshipped there as a pre-puberty small girl. She is offered a totally vegetarian diet so that her purity is maintained. The devotees visiting this temple regularly firmly believe that this deity does not allow anyone to go empty-handed. They believe that she listens to the prayers of all. Many have seen her blinking her eyes. The head priests who worship her regularly have also felt that on totally dark, moonless nights, she traverses the entire temple premises and, sometimes, she even talks in a whispering voice. *The dark matter of the idol gets transformed into dark energy.* (Reference 10)

References

[1] "Kamalakanta Bhattacharya (Bengal)" – *Wikipedia.*

[2] The song by Kamalakanta: "Jano Na Re Mon, Parama Karon", *Ananda Moyee* (on Facebook), 27th December 2017.

[3] "Sri Ramakrishna's First Ecstasy: White Cranes Against A Black Sky" – A Video Presentation on YouTube 2017, *neuralsurfer* Channel.

[4] "Sri Ramakrishna's First Samadhi Experience, Parts 1, 2 & 3," Video Presentations on YouTube, *Hindu Academy* Channel, 1st, 5th & 6th April 2024.

[5] "What does Sri Ramakrishna mean by going into the black water? Samadhi: Plunge Into Black Water" Video Presentation by Swami Sarvapriyananda on YouTube, Vedanta Society of New York. 15th July 2024.

[6] Shasthipada Chattopadhyay, *Dwadas Jyotirlinga*, (In Bengali); Kolkata: Orange Publishers, 2023.

[7] Swami Saradananda, *Sri Sri Ramakrishna Lila Prasanga, Part 1, Sadhak Bhav* (In Bengali), Kolkata: Udbodhan Karjalaya, 1993, p. 56.

[8] "Vishnu Puran: Know why Lord Vishnu took the Kurma Avatar" *Mind & Soul; Times Now Digital*; 28th May 2020.

[9] Paul J. Zak, *The Moral Molecule: How Trust Works*, New York: A Plume Book (Penguin Group), 2013.

[10] "Ma Shyamasundari of Kolkata" (In Bengali), *Anandabazar Online*, Ananda Utsab, 2024.

CHAPTER 5

Hinduism: Darkness

[In Hinduism, *sadhus* and *yogis* – at a very advanced stage of their *sadhana*, go for *Nirvikalpa Samadhi* when the brain waves become super-slow following the range of 0+ to 4 *hertz* (or cycles per second) when the mind becomes 'blank' – absolutely *dark*. So, *darkness* has a very special place in the practice of a high level of Hinduism. A realized and liberated *yogi* or *yogini* who has attained the level of *Nirvikalpa Samadhi* can consciously exit from their body and attain liberation at the moment of death while in a deep, conscious meditative state and get immersed into the *black hole* of *darkness*. Presumably, this is what had happened to both Sri Krishna Chaitanya Mahaprabhu and Sri Sri Ramakrishna. *Nirvikalpa Samadhi* is a state where no 'anchor' remains – no desire, no attachment and not even God. The moment the *yogi/yogini* gets 'anchored' during her/his *Nirvikalpa Samadhi*, the consciousness comes back like a spring. This is why Totapuri got utterly surprised when Ramakrishna did not even come back into consciousness even after being in *Nirvikalpa Samadhi* for three consecutive days. He had to be shouted back into consciousness. That was a sign of Thakur's *avatarhood*.]

Dark Matter & Dark Energy in Hinduism

99% of the 'Cosmos' (*'Brahmanda'*) is unmanifest – not conscious of anything – thus totally unattached to anything. This state endows it with tremendous power – ABSOLUTELY PURE POWER. Since we do not know anything about it, it appears DARK to us. In yogic culture, this unmanifested cosmos is referred as 'KAALA'.

In our language, 'Kaala' means 'black'; and, in Hinduism, although 'black' is considered inauspicious, Gods themselves have called the colour 'black' the supreme colour, since it represents the infinite expanse of the universe (that is, 'dark matter' and 'dark energy' in terms of astrophysics); it is *Parabrahman* itself. It is a symbol of 'wealth' (the *mangalsutra* is black). 'Black' is the colour of Saturn – *Shani Dev*, the god of justice. Among the other Hindu deities, out of the 9 forms of Nav Durga, the 7th form is *Mahakali.* So, Goddess Kali is black, Bhagawan Sri Krishna is deep blue (blackish tint), the Shaligram Stone (the form of Lord Vishnu, used in Hindu rituals and is believed to bring good luck, prosperity, and blessings to those who worship) is black and, of course, Shiva Linga is black. In Hindu culture, a black cow is considered more divine and is regarded as *Gau Mata.* Similarly, black ants are sober and positively charged than the red ones. (References 1 & 2)

Thus, 'kaala' has two dimensions: (i) TIME which is 'infinite'; and (ii) SPACE which is also 'infinite'. Whatever you cannot see as it does not stop 'light' (something which stops 'light'; we can see because it reflects 'light') is viewed as 'dark' ('kaala' in Indian language).

In India, there are two aspects of 'kaala'.

The 'time' dimension of 'kaala' is also expressed as 'kal' colloquially. It really has no bounds – it is eternal ('*ananta*' in Sanskrit'). The feminine gender of 'kal' is 'kali' and that is how the dark or black Hindu goddess is called. Goddess Kali, commonly known as *Ma* (Bengali for 'Mother') *Kali*, represents, as the American Kali-devotee William Clark says: 'the great womb of *time* itself, from which all emerges and to which all returns'.

'Kaala' means 'darkness' or 'black' which is related to 'space'. 'Kaala' also means 'time'. It should thus be interesting to note that 'time' is the basis of 'space'. For us humans, birth-death-rebirth cycle is thus very much related to this time-space conundrum (confusing apparently). Only because there is 'time', the distance between a point A and another point B is possible. Because there is a distance (which is a 'space' factor), we can measure 'time' on a clock or watch. The arms of the clock move over distances and provides us with the measurement of time in hours, minutes and seconds.

Incidentally, Lord Kelvin, who is regarded in the domain of physical sciences as the 'Master of Measurement' missed the measurement of time; instead, he measured 'temperature'.

Because there is 'time', 'distance' is possible and 'space' is possible. So, one word 'kaala' is good enough to represent 'time' as well as 'space', both.

In Sanskrit language, unmanifested existence is called 'SHI-VA'. 'SHI-VA' means 'that which is not' – in other words, 'that which is not manifest'. Now, most interestingly, this 'that which is not' or 'that which is not manifest' not only wakes up but becomes aggressively active when it gets stimulated by some amount of 'energy' or 'shakti'. So, we get the 'Shiva-Shakti' or 'Purusha-Prakriti' concept of Vedic or Tantric Hinduism. When 'Shi-va' got energized with 'Shakti', he took the form of an ellipsoid – he became erect. And, that is the concept of 'Shiva Linga'. 'Shi-va' was unmanifest; but when energized by 'Shakti', it became RUDRA. When 'Shi-va' settled down from his 'Rudra Rupa', he had many manifestations, which we refer to as CREATIONs. 'Creation' again is of two forms: one is 'pro-creation' – which is 'biological creation'; the other is 'intellectual creation'. 'Biological Creations' follow the space-time rule: 'birth-death-rebirth' cycle.

High level of authentic, original 'Intellectual Creations' do not follow the -'birth-death-rebirth (reprint/copying/new edition)' cycle. Such creations attract scholars to do further studies/investigation/interpretation/extension on the original work. Lord Kelvin used to believe that 'Science Is Measurement'. He had done colossal work on various types of measurements including the age of the Sun and the Earth. Lord Kelvin's original work on 'Dark Matter' & 'Dark Energy' have been followed up and refined by many physical scientists including Albert Einstein and, later on, by Stephen Hawking etc. Today, we know that all planets and stars are moving in the vast ocean of DARK ENERGY. The whole universe is thus SHIVA TATTVA. (References 3–6)

The First Humans: Dark-skinned

The first modern humans (*Homo Sapiens*) evolved from apes about 200,000 years ago in Africa. They were all dark-skinned. Some researchers suggest that human population over the past 50,000 years have changed from dark-skinned to light-skinned; and that such major changes in pigmentation may have happened in as little as 100 generations (that is, approximately, 2,500 years). (References 7–9)

The Birth of Ramakrishna: A Fair-skinned Child with Dark Energy

Ramakrishna's father Kshudiram, during his trip to Gaya had witnessed a *dream* where the four-handed Lord Vishnu appeared in front of him, most unexpectedly. (As Lord Vishnu holds a mace in one hand, he is also known as *Gadadhar*). Vishnu said he was too pleased with Kshudiram's *unconditional* (most important) devotion and also that He would very much like to be born in his family as his son. Kshudiram was awe-struck. Being overwhelmed, he said that he was a poor priest and will not be able to take proper care of the God if comes to him as his son. Vishnu smiled at him and said He will be too happy in whatever way Kshudiram and his wife managed to serve him. And, without waiting for Kshudiram's response, He disappeared.

Lord Vishnu, as I have already said had descended on earth as the *Kurma Avatar* and the land on which the Dakshineswar temple complex was constructed was of the shape of the hump of a tortoise. Sri Krishna was the eighth incarnation (*avatar*) of Lord Vishnu.

Krishna is pure *dark energy* (totally 'unattached' to anything). When a devotee surrenders to Sri Krishna, he also acquires *dark energy* and becomes eternally *liberated* (that is, free from all attachments). We become conditioned on account of our desire to enjoy materialistic way of life. A normal child born of such conditioned parents is thus conditioned and not liberated. Gadadhar (the birth name of Sri Sri Ramakrishna), since he was a form of Lord Vishnu (and thus Lord Krishna), he was born with *dark energy* and liberated, unattached –

although he was brimming with unconditional love for everyone. He was a fair-skinned child with *dark energy*.

Another incident contributed to Gadadhar's *dark energy*. A luminous ray had entered into Gadadhar's mother Chandradevi's body from the dark Shiva Linga installed in a Shiva temple close to her home in Kamarpukur. It was nothing else but *dark energy* as it originated from the dark Shiva Linga.

Having acquired *dark energy* from two divine sources (the Krishna *avatar* of Lord Vishnu and Shiva Linga), baby Gadadhar was naturally attracted towards *dark energy*. So, when the dark Goddess Kali appeared in his life at Dakshineswar, he was automatically attracted towards Her. (References 10 & 11)

Dark Matter in the Human Brain & Body

What makes the stars, the planets, and the galaxies staying together in the universe, is the *dark matter*. Similarly, what makes our *neurons* or brain cells staying together are the *synapses* that are responsible for the cell-to-cell connections and the *glial cells*. Unlike *neurons*, the *glial cells* in the brain are purely for support and are incapable of communication with each other. Thus, the *glial cells* constitute the *dark matter* of the human brain. In the past fifteen years, it has been discovered that **the *glial cells* are involved in many parts of cognition and memory**. The ratio of *glia* to *neurons* varies considerably from one region of the brain to another, although earlier it used to be believed that *glia* outnumbered *neurons* by 10:1 (or more). In the case of the brain of a person, who has never gone to school and never been exposed even to alphabets, it is only logical that the *glia* will outnumber the *neurons* to a large extent; and, if that be so it will it being the *dark matter* of the brain will attract *dark energy* from the universal soul (*paramatma*). Could that have been the case with *avatar* Sri Sri Ramakrishna?

The *Substantia Nigra* (*SN*) is a 'basal ganglia' structure located in the 'midbrain'. It plays an important and most critical role in the 'reward' functions (linked with the 'feel good' neuro-chemical *Dopamine* release) and modulation of movement towards the object of 'reward'. The term '*Substantia nigra*' is Latin for 'black substance' due to high levels of the *neuromelanin* in the *dopaminergic neurons*, playing a protective role. (*Neuromelanin* is a dark substance present in dark body hair and skin.) The *substantia nigra* also serves as a major source of *GABAergic* inhibition to various brain targets. *GABA* (*Gamma-aminobutyric acid*) is the neurotransmitter in the brain that slows down the brain by blocking specific signals in the Central Nervous System (CNS) (brain and the spinal cord) and produces a 'calming effect'. This explains Sri Sri Ramakrishna's strategy for *Dopamine Fasting* (*DF*) whenever it was called for.

The energy consumed by the brain when it is in the *Default Mode Network* (*DMN*) mode is about 20 times that used by the brain when it responds consciously to a mosquito or a fly or to any other outside stimulus. 60 to 80 percent of all energy used by the brain occurs in circuits unrelated to any external event. This intrinsic activity is carried out by the brain's *dark energy* – a reference to the unseen energy that represents the mass of the universe. This is the *neural dark energy*. Less energy is consumed by the brain when it is in the '*Task Performance Mode*' or when the '*Task Mode Network*' ('*TMN*') is engaged. When the *DMN* is engaged there is no 'Return on the Investment' (ROI) of the energy expended. Since Ramakrishna's brain was always in the *TMN* mode, he did not have that problem of wastage of precious neural energy.

A little over two decades ago, an enormous scientific effort revealed something most unexpected. It revealed that the human genome (that is, the 'gene pool') contains only 20,000 to 25,000 useful and productive protein-coding genes – which accounts for only 2% of our DNA. The rest was written off as 'junk' – but now it is coming to light that the balance 98% has a crucial role to play. It is our DNA's *dark matter*, known as the 'dark genome'. Experts now claim that this 'dark genome' helps to control how our genes behave in response to all the environmental pressures our bodies face throughout our lives, ranging from diet to stress, pollution, exercise, and how much we sleep, a field now known as *epigenetics*. It is now clear how Sri Sri Ramakrishna's 'dark genome' helped him to cope with his painstaking *sadhana* for months and years without anything to eat and no sleep. However, since we are only 10% human, and 90% microbial, due to the *avatar's* unbalanced lifestyle (with regard to diet and sleep), his health got affected as the microbiome is composed of *dark matter. Microbial Dark Matter (MDM)* comprises the vast majority of microbial organisms (usually *bacteria* and *archaea*) that microbiologists are unable to culture in the laboratory, due to lack of knowledge or ability to supply the required growth conditions. *MDM* is analogous to the *dark matter* of physics and cosmology due to its elusiveness in research and importance to the understanding of biological diversity. It is difficult to estimate the relative magnitude of *MDM*, but the accepted gross estimate is that as little as only one to two percent of microbial species in a given ecological niche is culturable. (References 12–20)

References

[1] T.N. Lifestyle Desk, "Why is the Mangalasutra Black, Despite the Colour Being Considered Inauspicious?" *TIMESNOW*, 4th May 2024.

[2] "Ram Temple: What is Shaligram Stone? Know religious significance here", *The Economic Times*, 31st January 2023.

[3] "Kaala – The Power of Darkness" Video Presentation by Sadhguru on YouTube, Sadhguru Channel.

[4] "What is the spiritual aspect of 'Dark Energy'?" Talk by Gurudev Sri Sri Ravi Shankar, Video Presentation on YouTube, Art of Living Channel.

[5] William Clark, "Is my Mother Shyama Black? A Song of Kamalakanta" *Kali Bhakti: An Offering for Our Divine Mother*; kalibhakti.com, 9th May 2019.

[6] A Movie titled, "Kelvin – Master of Measurement", You Tube 10 April, 2017.

[7] Michael Muehlenbein, *Human Evolutionary Biology*, Cambridge: Cambridge University Press, 2010, pp. 192–213.

[8] Nina Jablonski and George Chaplain, "The colours of humanity: the evolution of pigmentation in the human lineage", *Philosophical Transactions of the Royal Society,* May 2017, Vol. 372, Issue/No. 172420160349.

[9] Nina G. Jablonski, "Why Human Skin Comes in Colors (PDF)", ArthroNotes Vol. 32, No. 1, Retrieved 2013-07-20; Archived (PDF) from the original on 2014-02-25.

[10] Parth Khajgiwale, "Attachment is an illusion: Exploring the Concept in the Bhagavad Gita", *Readers' Blog*, Indiatimes.com, 27th May 2023.

[11] HDG A.C. Bhaktivedanta Swami Prabhupada, "Jesus was an empowered incarnation of Krishna", *Krishna.Org*, 6th February 2023.

[12] Ethan Siegel, "This is How Much Dark Matter Passes Through Your Body Every Second", *Forbes*, 3rd July, 2018.

[13] "Glial Cells: The 'Dark Matter' of the Brain", *BrainInjury.com*

[14] "The dark matter of the brain", *Max Planck Geselllschaft*, 5th April 2022.

[15] "Substantia nigra" – *Wikipedia.*

[16] Luigi Zecca, David Sulzer, "Neuromelanin of the substantia nigra: A neuronal black hole with protective and toxic characteristics", *Trends in Neurosciences*, 2003. (Also refer to 'Neuromelanin', *Science Direct, sciencedirect.com*).

[17] "Gamma-Aminobutyric Acid (GABA)", *Cleveland Clinic*, last reviewed on 25th April 2022.

[18] David Cox, "The mystery of the human genome's dark matter", *BBC*, 13th April 2023.

[19] "Microbial dark matter" – *Wikipedia.*

[20] Marcus E. Raichle, "The Brain's Dark Energy" *Scientific American*, March 2010, Vol. 302, No. 3.

CHAPTER 6

Ramakrishna: A Striking Example of 'Dark Energy'

"Just Because You Haven't Seen It, Doesn't Mean It Doesn't Exist."

—**Pierce Brown,** from his 2019 book *Dark Age,* New York: Del Ray (Penguin Random House)

Dark Energy is formless (*nirakar* in Sanskrit). When *dark energy* descends on earth from the cosmos, it manifests itself not just in one form (*sakar* in Sanskrit), it takes many forms. And, that was what Sri Sri Ramakrishna was. He appeared in many forms. That was one characteristic of his *avatarhood.* Swami Vivekananda was handsome, but his energy never got manifested in many forms. He was one having a high order of *divya bhava* (post-human propensities), but not an *avatar.*

Once a devotee had asked Thakur Ramakrishna whether God had a form (*sakar*) or He was formless (*nirakar*) and, he had answered in his usual story-telling way. He had said: "There was a chameleon on top of a tree. One person found it to be of green colour. Another one said that he had found it to be black. A third person found it to be yellow and a fourth one said he had found it to be green. Like this, different people found the same lizard but in different colours. Having different perceptions, they started arguing with each other. Then they found one person sitting under the big shady tree. As he said that he lived there, they asked him about the colour of the lizard. He said, the creature was a chameleon. It changed its colour from time to time and sometimes it cannot be seen as it becomes almost colourless so that it cannot be seen and detected by predating big birds like kites and eagles."

Ramakrishna was a person of multiple *bhavas*. He had multiple faiths and beliefs -totally unbiased – *attached* to none. He had conquered and transcended his 'Small Ego' for ever. This is a typical manifestation of *dark energy*. Because Thakur had attained *astasiddhi*, at times he could become very small and, at other times, too big – unimaginably big. Sometimes, he would have dishevelled hair and very little cover on his body; and, at some other times, very well-dressed in his dhoti, black coat, and polished black shoes. Sometimes, one would have found him in deep trance – *samadhi*; and, at some other times, he would be moving very fast with long steps. However, he was against such demonstration of his *siddhai* powers, lest common people were afraid of visiting him and coming close to him for his blessings. He used to pray to the Mother Goddess to stop manifesting such powers through him. He wanted to mix with everyone and not to maintain a distance from anyone. He was very keen on manifestation of his inner, and not his outer powers.

Gadadhar's divine existence could be felt by many from his pre-teen and teen days. In his village Kamarpukur, the zamindar was Dharmadas Laha. His widowed daughter Prasanna used to regard him as Gadadhar (Lord Vishnu) in the human form. While listening to his informal talks full of stories from the Hindu *puranas* and his devotional songs, this simple-hearted lady used to be mesmerised and she used to ask him: "Oh, Gadai! Can you tell me why, at times, I feel that you are none else than someone who has descended from the heavenly abode of gods and goddesses? Yes, really, I can't think of you, other than somebody who has come from high above." Young Gadadhar used to smile and laugh it off, but Prasanna had never changed her opinion about him.

Let us not confuse *dark energy* with *tamo guna*. *Dark energy* is an ideal combination of all the three *gunas* – *sattva, rajas* and *tamas*. Goddess Kali can drink the blood of the *asuras* that she slays – which is *tamas*. She is highly active in fighting the *asuras* and killing them – *rajas*. And, she is also the protector of the pure and innocent people who have unconditional love in their hearts – *sattva*.

In us, the humans, for any *tamasic* activity (*poshu bhava*), there is *adrenalin* rush from the *adrenal* glands located near the kidneys. For the action-oriented *rajasic* propensities (*veera* or *naro bhava*), the brain has a rush of the neurotransmitter *acetylcholine*. And, for the *sattvic* pure, unconditional love (*divya bhava*), the brain releases *oxytocin* from the brain's *pituitary glands.*

Sri Sri Ramakrishna and '*Dark Energy*'

Goddess Kali is a *dark goddess*. And, whatever material the idol may be made of – whether it is clay, stone, or metal, it would be *dark matter.* When the image (*murti*) of any deity is installed in a new or existing temple, a highly trained *siddha* priest has to perform certain rituals (including chanting *mantras,* performing *mudras*) according to the scriptures to infuse life (*pran pratistha*) into the idol.

For infusing life into a *dark goddess* made of *dark matter,* you need most uncommon, very special *dark energy*. The usual forms of energy, (i) 'physical' such as light, heat, electricity, magnetism, wind; or (ii) 'chemical', etc. will not serve the purpose. Moreover, even if an experienced '*siddha*' priest does the *pran pratistha* initially, the regular worshipping priest (*pujari*) gets nothing but a dead, deaf-and-dumb idol.

When Sri Sri Ramakrishna took over the *pujari* role from his elder brother Ramkumar and started worshipping the *Dark Goddess* regularly, he used to engage himself into various sports (*leela*) with the Goddess, like talking, feeding her, sharing *bhog* and *prasad* with her, jumping on to her lap, sleeping on her cot etc. These were all possible with the help of *dark energy* which he had acquired at the time of his birth.

While on a trip to Gaya, Ramakrishna's father Kshudiram had witnessed a dream in which Lord Vishnu talked to him and said that he will be born as his son. The *dark god* Sri Krishna was the eighth *avatar* of Vishnu who was also dark-skinned. So, that was one source of *dark energy* for Sri Sri Ramakrishna.

Ramakrishna's mother had experienced a flow of energy entering into her body from the Shiva temple near her house. *Shiva Linga* is *dark* and thus a source of *dark energy.* (References 1 & 2)

A Song on the Dark Goddess

"Is my mother Shyama black?
People say that Kali means black, but my
mind says that this is not so.
In Her dark beauty, the Naked One
Illuminates the lotus of my heart.

Is my mother Shyama black?
Shyama is sometimes white, at other times yellow,
again blue, and vibrant red

The Mother's true nature is beyond my understanding
and in contemplating Her my life has dissolved

Is my mother Shyama black?
Shyama is sometimes spirit, sometimes matter,
and the transcendent void beyond both
Lost in her ecstasy, Kamalakanta has gone insane.

Is my mother Shyama black?"

This devotional song, composed by a famous Bengali *tantrik* adept named Kamalakanta Bhattacharya (1769–1829) (and translated in English by William Clark), by chance (I don't think 'by choice'), talks about the link between the *dark* goddess and the *dark matter* and *dark energy* that constitutes the bulk of our cosmos.

I get the feeling that the poet and songwriter has compared Mother Kali with the cosmos (*brahmanda*). Like the naked Goddess ('*digambari*' in Bengali), the space above us – the entire cosmos is 'naked' and its beauty is unique and unparalleled. It looks black at night with only the little stars twinkling like the fireflies (Ramakrishna and Narendra Nath used to have such visions at the initial stage of their meditation). During the day when the sun is out, the sky above changes colour. At the moment of sunrise, the sky is vibrant red. Then, as the sun moves and the day progresses, the sky changes its colour to blue and then yellow, as the poet says. With the clouds passing, the sky may appear white.

The goddess, if we imagine her as a living one, she would have a 'gross body' which is 'matter'; and, she would also have a 'subtle body' which is the 'spirit' or 'soul'. So, the *tantrik* poet is in doubt whether Mother Shyama (alias Ma Kali) is really black.

Like in the case of all work of art, the interpretation of the song is in the mind of the reader!! (Reference 3)

A Case of Positive Awe-inspiring Experience Provided by Sri Sri Ramakrishna

Looking at the vast expanse of *dark* sky inspires *awe* in us. A similar striking *awe-inspiring* experience one has by getting exposed to the image of the *dark* Goddess Kali. Of late, in the realm of psychology, Dacher Keltner, professor at the University of California, Berkeley and his colleagues have taken out the emotion of *awe* from the back bench and placed it on the front row through extensive cross-cultural research. A positive *awe*-inspiring experience can release the 'feel good' neurotransmitter *Dopamine* ('*D*').

[*Awe* is the ability to revere things, to regard things as sacred. Positive *awe* is a spiritual emotion and is responsible for releasing the neurotransmitter *'Oxytocin'* ('*O*').]

I am taking this opportunity to share a case where Sri Sri Ramakrishna himself provided an awe-inspiring experience to someone who had no idea of his superior spirituality. In this case, the trust molecule *'Oxytocin'* ('*O*') would have been released in the brain of the person with whom he was interacting.

A brahmin scholar Shyamapada Nyayabagish (SN, in short) once came to Ramakrishna's small room adjacent to the Dakshineswar temple. Through the door, he looked inside before entering. Finding his simple cot, beddings and very ordinary lifestyle, SN wondered what kind of a *Paramhansa* this man was. He entered straight into the room with his shoes on and asked with a lot of vanity: "Where is the *Paramhansa*?" A few devotees were present in the room. They pointed towards Thakur who was sitting on his cot. SN moved towards Thakur and sat on his cot without seeking his consent. Then he asked most egoistically:

"Are you the *Paramhansa*? Nobody will believe by just looking at you." Then he said: "OK! Tell me how you have *managed* to attain such a status. After having studied so many scriptures for so many years, I am still struggling to make both ends meet, and you are in a most joyful mood having come to be known as the *Paramhansa*".

Ramakrishna, most humorously, pointed to the other trivial items present in the room like a water pot and so on and asked SN to take note of those also. The devotees present, all, broke into silent, soundless laughter.

SN asked: "How have you *managed* to influence so many people. You're spoiling your own future by faking your identity as a *sadhu*; but why are you spoiling the future of so many people by brainwashing them, giving them a wrong message?" After having made a few more derogatory remarks, he started sharing with those present his own perception of *Paramhansa*, quoting from different scriptures. However, when he did not get much positive response from Thakur's devotees, he left the room.

In the evening, he went to the riverside for his evening prayers and worship. And, Thakur also came out of his room, walking a little here and there, went to the riverside, and then went back to his room. He suddenly went into *bhava* and started chanting god's name by dancing at the same time.

And, as far as SN was concerned, he was not getting the image of his *ishta devata* during his meditation. Instead, every time, the image of Sri Sri Ramakrishna was flashing on his mind's screen. Much though he tried again and again, but he simply could not remove Thakur's image from his mind. This was indeed an *awe*-inspiring experience for him – a highly positive one, totally unexpected by him and that changed him. The trust molecule *Oxytocin* started getting released from his brain's *'Pituitary Gland'* (*'PiG'*) which helped him to believe that Ramakrishna was not just an ordinary *sadhu*, he was indeed a *Paramhansa*.

Once he had such a realisation, he ran to Thakur's room and touched his feet in great respect. Thakur, in his *bhava* mood, shouted and placed his right foot right on top of SN's head. SN was also overwhelmed in joy; tears started flowing down both his cheeks, which helped to erase all the negative attitude and behaviour that he had displayed with Thakur a few hours earlier. (References 4–8)

Sri Sri Ramakrishna: Inseparable from Goddess Kali

Matter is defined as anything that has a mass and occupies space. So, the basalt stone image of the black goddess at Dakshineswar was nothing else but *dark matter*, as it had a mass and it occupied space. 'Fairness' is the opposite of 'darkness' and, because opposites attract each other, Goddess Kali was so much drawn to the fair-skinned Lord Shiva and also to Her fair-skinned young priest Gadadhar. Gadadhar, on his part also, was mad about the dark goddess. Let me share three stanzas of a beautiful pop song 'Opposites Attract' by Paula Abdul:

"Baby, it seems we never, ever agree
You like the movies and I like the TV
I take things serious and you take 'em light
I go to bed early and I party all night

Our friends are sayin' we ain't going to last
'Cause I move slowly and baby, I'm fast
I like it quiet and I love to shout
But when we get together, it just all works out

I take a-two steps forward, I take two steps back
We come together 'cause *opposites attract*
And you know it ain't fiction, just a natural fact
We come together 'cause *opposites attract.*"

(italics mine; songwriter: Oliver J. Leiber)

In his early days with Sri Sri Ramakrishna, Narendra Nath had never believed in the presence and power of the *Dark Goddess* as he used to attend the meetings of *Brahmo Samaj* and interact regularly with the great thinkers like Maharshi Debendranath Tagore and Keshab Chandra Sen. The *Brahmos* are non-believers in God having a form ('*sakar*' in Sanskrit). In other words, they believe in the *energy* only, and not in the *matter,* whereas Thakur believed that the Goddess was a living entity, just like a human being – an integrated form of *matter* and *energy* both. For Thakur, it took six long years to change Naren's belief. Eventually, Naren was more than convinced that there was a strong connection between the Goddess and Thakur; that both were inseparable and both were living.

As Swami Vivekananda, he had once mentioned to Sister Nivedita: "Nivedita, you've a feeling that in future, there is a strong possibility that people will regard Ramakrishna as an incarnation of the *Dark Goddess* Kali herself, isn't it? When I come to think of it, I don't tend to disagree with you. It is not unlikely that the Mother Goddess had Herself descended on Earth in the body of Thakur."

Incident One

One personal experience had been shared by Rakhal (who later became Swami Brahmananda). He talked about a time when he used to visit Thakur from Baranasi Ghosh Street. One day when he had gone to Dakshineswar in the early afternoon, Ma Kali's temple was closed and Thakur was taking rest after lunch. As soon as Rakhal reached, Thakur asked him to sit on his bed and requested him to massage his feet. Rakhal refused by saying: "Spare me please! Is there anyone available to massage my feet? Please give up that idea. Let us continue to chat like earlier." However, when Thakur kept insisting by saying: "You get blessed if you take good care of a *sadhu*." Once he repeated this message two three times and Rakhal just touched his feet about to apply massage, he witnessed no less than a miracle. He saw the Mother Goddess entering into the room in the form of a pre-teen girl wearing anklets. She circled round Thakur's cot three-four times at a very fast pace, then disappeared into his chest. Thakur said to Rakhal smilingly: "Did you see the result of taking care of a *sadhu*? It came instantly." Rakhal could not believe what he had just witnessed. It was absolutely unbelievable.

Incident Two

Towards the end of 1885, Ramakrishna shifted to Shyampukur for his treatment. Just one day before Kali Puja, Thakur instructed some of his devotees to make all arrangements for the puja next day. The devotees were only too happy to complete all arrangements. However, the day was gone and evening came. Thakur was not mentioning anything about the puja; he was still sitting on his bed. Finding this, the devotees started cleaning up some space towards his eastern side and placed all the provisions that they had organised for the purpose of puja. This they did based on their earlier experience when they had found that he had worshipped himself as an embodiment of the Goddess. Thakur did not object, nor did he pass any comment when the devotees were taking such actions.

After a little while, when all such arrangements were complete, lamps had been lit and incense sticks had been lighted, still there was no action on the part of Thakur. He was still sitting in a most relaxed posture. Along with the young devotees, Sri M, Ram Chandra, Debendranath and Girish Chandra were also present. Girish Chandra suddenly had a brain wave. He thought Thakur must be expecting the devotees to worship him as an integral part of the Mother Goddess. He became ecstatic with this thought, collected some flowers, took some sandalwood paste and offered at the feet of Thakur by uttering 'Jai Ma!' Thakur's whole body trembled and he entered into *samadhi*. His face displayed a luminous aura, and most gracefully he used the protective *mudra* following the style of Mother Goddess. All this happened most suddenly and all present saw Girish offering Thakur *anjali* again and again. Those who were sitting or standing a little away from Thakur could witness as if Thakur had appeared before them in the form and style of Mother Jagattarini.

Incident Three

Ramakrishna was once in the Cossipore garden house. His illness had taken a very bad turn. Ma Sarada was in a tensed mood. Suddenly she found the *dark goddess* with long dark hair came close to Thakur and sat on his bed.

Sarada exclaimed: "Oh, Mother! You've come?"

Ma Kali: "Yes! Just now I came from Dakshineswar."

After exchange of some words and messages, Sarada saw Goddess Kali was sitting with Her neck bent as if she was in pain.

Sarada asked: "Oh, Mother! Why have you bent your neck? Are you in pain?"

Ma Kali: "Yes, my girl! I have burning sore in my throat."

Sarada: "My husband has been suffering from some sore in his throat. Is it the same with you too?"

Ma Kali: "Yes, dear!"

Sarada could realise that Thakur and the Mother Goddess were one. They were one soul comprising *dark energy*, in two different bodies: one dark-skinned and the other fair-skinned.

Sri Sri Ramakrishna: Inseparable from Lord Shiva

In Gadadhar's native village Kamarpukur, there used to be *jatra* performance every year on the occasion of *Shiva Ratri*. The village folks had decided to put up a play dealing with Lord Shiva's glory. Unfortunately, the play was about to be cancelled as the boy who was supposed to perform in the role of the pre-teen Shiva had been down with some illness all of a sudden. Gadai had agreed to play the role on such a short notice at the request of the village seniors.

Gadai was thinking about Shiva in the dressing room, all dressed up like pre-teen Shiva, when he was called to appear on stage. A friend of his came along to show him the way. He stood up at his friend's instance, and slowly went to the stage, totally absent-minded, without paying attention to anything around. He stood there still, without moving a bit. Finding young Gadai dressed up in the pre-teen Shiva's attire with matted hair and loin cloth and being impressed with his divine looks, the members of the audience were so overwhelmed with joy and surprise that they started shouting the name of *Lord Hara* (that is, *Shiva*) in the typical village style. Some of the women present started playing the conch. The programme director began chanting the *Shiva Stuti* to calm down the audience. It helped in reducing the excitement a little but there were still people appreciating the dressed-up Gadai.

Some were saying that they had never expected that Gadai will be fitting into that role so well. Some shouted saying that we must form a theatre troupe by including Gadai to play the lead roles.

Despite all this going on in the background, Gadai continued to stand still as if nothing has happened. There were tears rolling down his cheeks incessantly. When some people found that the boy was speechless and that he was not moving, they went and touched him to find that his limbs were almost paralysed. Young Gadai had lost his senses. The crowd became restless. Some suggested water to be sprinkled on his face. Some others started fanning him with a hand fan. While some others said that the boy had spoiled the entire play. As a matter of fact, the play was cancelled and some of Gadai's well-wishers carried him on their shoulders. It is said that the boy did not regain his consciousness until sunrise.

One day, Thakur, while in a highly spiritual mood, had told Swami Brahmananda that the Shiva in him was not a stationery one like the one installed in a temple, on the floor. His Shiva had originated from under the ground itself. It was like the rains of the monsoon; came in full force, then disappeared. What he wanted to say was that the Shiva mood was not a permanent feature with him. It came at times on some provocation and then suddenly disappeared. He was a man of many moods.

Swami Saradananda has written in great detail about what Baikunthanath had once witnessed in Thakur. Thakur was telling Baikunthanath: "See! Once Bamni (Bhairavi Ma), Baishnav Charan, Gouri Pandit, the court scholar of Burdwan Raj Padmalochan had all confirmed my *avatarhood.* Now, Girish, Ram, Monomohan – they all claim that I am an *avatar.* I've got utterly bored and disgusted by hearing that I am an *avatar.* I say, what do you think – how do you feel about me?"

Baikunthanath said: "Those who say that you're an *avatar,* they know nothing."

Thakur: "All those people have regarded me as an *avatar*; and, you say – they know nothing. What do you mean, may I know?"

Baikunthanath: "My perception is that the *avatar* concept is not a complete one. It is only a part."

Thakur: "You're absolutely right! But what is your idea?"

Baikunthanath: "You are the complete *Shiva*, not just a part. I am firm about this because whenever I've tried to meditate on Lord Shiva as per your advice, every time I've witnessed you occupying my whole mental screen and nobody else. So, I'm convinced that you're Shiva – you're *Satyam Shivam Sundaram*!"

Thakur: "You're not wrong in your perception, but if you ask me I'm nowhere near him – not even close to one hair of the Supreme Lord." Thakur broke into loud laughter.

The Conjoined Twins in Spiritual Thought

'Shiva' and 'Shakti', 'Purusha' and 'Prakriti' are like conjoined twins in the Hindu spiritual thought. Rani Rashmoni's son-in-law Mathur Babu had witnessed the manifestation of both these *bhavas* in Thakur Sri Sri Ramakrishna.

Thakur, while he used to be alone, remained immersed in his own thoughts. One day, in such a state of mind, he was walking on the veranda at the north-east corner of his room in Dakshineswar. Mathur Babu was sitting alone in a room in the bungalow that was meant for the use of the Rani and her family members. It used to be known as the *Babuder Kuthi.* Since the room where Mathur Babu was sitting was not very far from the place where Thakur Ramakrishna was walking, it was very much in his line of vision. Mathur's mind was swinging between two streams of thought. On the one hand, his thoughts were totally materialistic about the Rani's estate, trade and business; on the other, he was thinking about Thakur and his religious and spiritual activities.

Thakur was not aware about Mathur Babu's presence in the *Babuder Kuthi.* It took him by total surprise when Mathur came running, prostrated before him, embraced both his feet and started crying. Thakur exclaimed: "What are you up to Sejo Babu? You are Rani Ma's son-in-law – why are you touching my feet. Please get up and hold yourself straight." Mathur was not in a mood to listen to him. He went on saying: "Baba! You were walking on the veranda and do you know what I saw? When you are coming forward, I could clearly see that it was not you – it was none else but the Mother Goddess of the temple and when you were going backward, I found Lord Shiva in your place. I wiped my eyes to ensure whether I was hallucinating or not – I did it not only once, but a few times, and every time I saw you in both the divine forms (*rupas*) – both Goddess Kali and Lord Shiva. You're not an ordinary person, Baba......you're someone very special."

Thakur reacted: "Well, Babu! I do not know or feel anything special. I'm getting scared instead. If this goes into the ears of Rani Ma....what will she think? She may think I must have used black magic with you."

Some sages and saints show miracles to common people to earn their faith and trust. Miracles help to release the trust molecule *'Oxytocin'* (*'O'*) in their brains. *Avatar* Ramakrishna was very much against showing miracles. His spiritual mother *Jagattarini Ma* helped him to externalise his 'Shiva Soul' and 'Kali Soul' separately during one of his *'bhava mukhs'* when he was in a mood which used to take him far away from the mundane materialistic world.

A 'White Hole' Overpowering A 'Black Hole'

A 'black hole' in the cosmos has extremely strong and most powerful negative energy which moves at the speed of light. It sucks and consumes everything that comes close to it in space-time. A 'white hole' is just the opposite. It spits and spews and ejects out energy from within in space-time. It has no negativity present in it and nothing can go inside it from outside. It is just the reverse of a 'black hole'.

Astronomers have been trying to study the behaviour of these two types of 'holes' very closely and they say that if a 'white hole' comes in contact or collides with a 'black hole', the latter will overpower it and win in the battle. So, the weaker 'white hole' is consumed by the 'black hole' which becomes larger in size. I will share a case study where Thakur Sri Sri Ramakrishna who can be compared to a very powerful 'white hole' changed the negative nature of a 'black hole' person.

Manmatha Bhattacharya was a branded villain. He was originally from Goswami Para of North Calcutta, but came to stay in his maternal uncle's house in Baghbazar. He was in the employment of the rich manager of a big landlord. Although he was a high-caste brahmin, he hardly had a brahmin-like lifestyle. He was very strong in constitution and used to build his body by taking heavy exercises regularly. His nature was very vindictive. Everyone in his locality used to be scared of him and whenever there was any fight, he was the first person who would intrude. He had the capacity to overpower all involved. For that reason, people used to refer to him as 'Manmatha Villain'. I compare him to a 'black hole' because of his very nature.

Strangely enough, once he was entrusted with the responsibility of scaring Ramakrishna Paramhansa. But, while he was about to carry out the task with which he had been entrusted, his life took a total turn. 'Manmatha Villain' turned into an ardent devotee of Thakur Ramakrishna. I will tell you what had actually happened.

Thakur had a devotee by the name of Jogin Ma. Her house was in Baghbazar. She had a brother by the name of Hiralal. Hiralal never liked Thakur and he never approved of her sister visiting him. However, Jogin Ma had a long-cherished desire to bring Thakur to her house. So, one day, she made all arrangements to translate her desire into reality. When her brother Hiralal came to know about her plans, he was most annoyed and his entire anguish was related to Thakur. He chalked out a strategy to scare Ramakrishna so that he would never wish to visit their house in future. Hiralal immediately thought of 'Manmatha Villain', got in touch and made a pact with him.

Manmatha was ready to perform the task assigned to him. Thakur arrived at Jogin Ma's house like a most luminous 'white hole' radiating his *aura*. The 'black hole' Manmatha met him face to face. There was an immediate *virtual* collision between the two 'holes' – the negative 'dark' and the highly positive 'white'. And, instead of taking his pre-planned actions to threaten Thakur, Manmatha's attitude took a total turn. He asked for forgiveness and, most surprisingly, he was so much overwhelmed with his '*awe*'-inspiring experience that tears started rolling down both his cheeks.

The merciful Thakur not only pardoned him, but he also asked him to visit Dakshineswar.

Manmatha went to Dakshineswar one day with Gangadhar (who later became Swami Akhandananda). When Gangadhar told Thakur about Manmatha's misdeeds, he examined his body with his right hand and took him aside to a desolate corner) by the side of the temple where he prayed for him quietly for some time and then let him go. The villain became a devout devotee and, thereafter, whenever he would visit Thakur in Dakshineswar, he would address him as 'My dearest!'.

Sri Sri Ramakrishna: Reincarnation of Sri Krishna Chaitanya

Sri Sri Ramakrishna, quite often, used to share one of his special *visions* with his devotees that he could identify himself with Sri Krishna, the eighth *avatar* of Lord Vishnu. He could clearly visualise that he was engaged in sport (*leela*) with the Gopis where they were transacting unconditional, *pure love* (which, in neuroscience, is represented by the brain chemical *Oxytocin – 'O'*, secreted from our brain's 'Pituitary Glands' – 'PiG'). The Gopis, on hearing Sri Krishna's flute used to leave everything – all their relations, kith and kin, and come out of their respective dwellings as if they had turned mad – such was the *Dark God*'s magnetic pull. Sri Krishna had no material wealth as such; still they loved Him more than themselves. The *Dark God* Sri Krishna acted as a most powerful *black hole* which had *sucked* the Gopis entirely in body, mind and soul which they had surrendered to him without thinking twice.

The lady ascetic Gouri Ma had cherished a desire to witness the sport (*leela*) of Sri Gouranga in the persona of Ramakrishna Paramhansa, but she had kept her desire to herself – did not express it to anyone. A few days later, her wish was fulfilled at the instance of the Paramhansa. It was a Sunday and Gouri Ma had cooked several items herself and came to Thakur at Dakshineswar. At about the same time, one of Thakur's devotees, Kedar Chatterjee was with him and Thakur was telling him about Gouri Ma. Kedar and Gouri Ma both were overwhelmed at this strange coincidence. Their eyes were filled with tears of divine happiness. Their happiness had infected Thakur also. He shared his meal with the devotees who were there including Rakhal and Ramchandra Dutta. All of a sudden those present found the presence of a *divine being* in Thakur's body. It was not difficult to make out that it was none other than Bhagawan Sri Krishna Chaitanya Mahaprabhu. The small room of Ramakrishna was filled with highly spiritual vibrations. This is what Gouri Ma had desired to witness and it did happen in front of her on that day, most unexpectedly for her.

Sri Gouranga, a most balanced combination of both Sri Krishna and Sri Radhika had a culmination of *madhura bhava* in him. In a similar way, Sri Sri Ramakrishna took the form of Sri Krishna at times and also of Sri Radha at some other times; and manifested the *madhura bhava*. It did not take him very long to get a *vision* of Radharani and he could very well feel that the figure of her got sucked into his body as if he acted like a *black hole*. He was so much engrossed into the thoughts of Sri Radhika that blood started oozing out of the pores of his skin. During such an experiencing phase, he simply could not think that he had a male body. He couldn't dream of it either. After a few days, he witnessed Lord Sri Krishna in a *vision* and, it did not take much time for the *Dark God* to be sucked into his own body. What a wonderful sport (*leela*) that Sri Sri Ramakrishna was engaged in!!

Ramakrishna Paramhansa used to get into *samadhi* by listening to the popular *kirtan*: (translation from Bengali into English is mine)

"The resident beauty of Vrindavan Rai is ours
The resident beauty of Vrindavan Rai is ours
Oh My Friend! Rai is ours, Rai is ours!
We belong to Rai, Shyam is yours
Rai is ours
Oh, My Friend! Rai is ours
We belong to Rai, Shyam is yours
Rai is ours!
The resident beauty of Vrindavan Rai is ours

The resident beauty of Vrindavan Rai is ours!
Shuk says – My Krishna's hair-crest is leaning to the left
And Shari says
And Shari says – As He desires to have the touch of Radha's feet
That is why the hair-crest leans to the left
That is why Krishna's hair-crest leans to the left
As He desires to have the touch of Radha's feet!
The resident beauty of Vrindavan Rai is ours
The resident beauty of Vrindavan Rai is ours!
Shuk says – The peacock's feather is on my Krishna's head
And Shari says
And Shari says – My Radha's name is written on it
But it cannot be seen
But it cannot be seen!
The resident beauty of Vrindavan Rai is ours
The resident beauty of Vrindavan Rai is ours!
The conflict between Shuk and Shari came to a close
The conflict between Shuk and Shari came to a close!
Joy, joy in the name of Radha-Krishna now
Oh, say Hari Hari in the name of Radha-Krishna now
And go to Vrindavan
Joy, joy Say Hari Hari in the name of Radha-Krishna now
And go to Vrindavan
The resident beauty of Vrindavan Rai is ours
The resident beauty of Vrindavan Rai is ours!
Oh, My Friend! Rai is ours, Rai is ours
We belong to Rai, Shyam is yours
Rai is ours
Oh My Friend! Rai is ours, Rai is ours
The resident beauty of Vrindavan Rai is ours!
The resident beauty of Vrindavan Rai is ours!"

If the two sexes (*'purusha'* and *'prakriti'*) are in different bodies, there may be misunderstanding, there may be conflict. But if the body is of one gender but the soul – the mood (*bhava*) is of the opposite gender, and if they are inter-dependent and well-coordinated and well-matched, chances of misunderstandings and conflicts are remote.

When the Paramhansa used to have the *prakriti bhava* manifested in him, he used to have some specific kinds of desires. He used to contemplate that the Gopis of Vrindavan had been born in the female gender which had helped them to win the love of Bhagawan Sri Krishna, how can he achieve the same goal having been born in the male gender. It would have been readily possible for him if he would have been born in the female gender (in the *'prakriti'* form). He used to feel, very strongly, that his male gender was certainly a barrier for winning over the grace of Lord Krishna. So, he used to think that if he was going to be born again, he would be born as a most beautiful girl, widowed at an early age, with flowing hair and would not accept anyone else as husband.

I will now tell you what had happened one day. There would be a Bhagavad reading session in the Dakshineswar temple. Thakur was sitting in the lobby in front of the Vishnu temple. While listening to the Bhagavad being read by a Pundit, he was totally absorbed. In that semi-conscious state, he had a divine *vision* of the luminous figure of Bhagawan Sri Krishna. A little while later, he found a ray of light came out from the lotus feet of Sri Krishna and fell on the sacred text of Srimad Bhagavad. Soon after, it came out of the sacred text and fell on himself. And, he sucked it readily like a *black hole*. That way, the luminosity integrated all the three things for some time: Bhagawan Sri Krishna, the sacred text Bhagavad, and Thakur Ramakrishna.

Thakur got an insight from this experience which he used to share later with his disciples and devotees that: Bhagawan, Bhagavad (the sacred text/scriptures) and the fully 'devoted' devotee are all integrated into one. They are not separate from each other.

There are a few more such instances when Thakur took the form of Sri Chaitanya Mahaprabhu in front of Gouri Ma about which I will tell you now.

Instance 1

For the very first time, Gouri Ma heard about Sri Sri Ramakrishna from an elderly person – Hare Krishna Mukhopadhyay. Hare Krishna said to her: "Oh! My Mother! I have just witnessed an extra-ordinary person today at Dakshineswar. So good-looking, so knowledgeable, so full of love! And, he loses his consciousness most frequently."

On her return from Puri, Gouri Ma became a guest of Ramakrishna devotee Balaram Basu. Balaram used to tell her every now and then: "Sister! I want you to meet that wonderful person. I do not want you to regret later that I missed the chance". Gouri Ma used to reply: "Brother! I've had the good fortune to be blessed by so many *sadhus*, I have no desire to meet any more of them. However, if your *sadhu* has the power to pull me towards him, then let him do so. I am not interested to meet him on my own."

One day, after performing her daily *puja*, she was humming a devotional song. And, as she was about to put her deity, the *Damodar Sila* back to his throne after she bathed and dressed him up, she found the throne was occupied with two living human feet. She first thought that it was an illusion. But when she saw the same sight again and again and when the *tulsi* leaf from her idol flew and fell on those two living feet, she lost her senses.

The whole day was spent like this. At night, in her sleep, she could hear a male voice talking to her in an emotional tone: "You'll not come to visit me, if I do not pull you?" She immediately asked: "Who are you? The sound of your voice seems so familiar." And, she got the reply: "Yes, of course! When you come to me, you'll recognise and know who I am. Why don't you come? Please come soon."

The very next day, early in the morning, Gouri Ma arrived at Dakshineswar with Balaram Basu. As she entered Ramakrishna's room, she found he was singing a song with his fingers being busy in winding a thread on a stick: "Ma Yashoda used to make me dance by addressing me as the 'Blue Gem' ('*Neel Moni*' in Bengali)! Where have you hidden that form, Oh, my Shyama Mother, Why don't you dance once?"

Most spontaneously, Gouri Ma went forward to touch Thakur's feet and, to her utter surprise, she found the same two feet which she had found on the throne of her *Damodar Sila*. She looked straight into Thakur's eyes and found him smiling. The Paramhansa said: "Please come again".

After a few days, Gouri Ma told a famous person: "There is no difference between my Guru Sri Sri Ramakrishna and Bhagawan Sri Krishna Chaitanya. Both are just the same!."

Actually, *dark energy* is transferable. Chaitanya Dev had *dark energy* from Sri Krishna of whom he was the *avatar* and Sri Sri Ramakrishna was also an excellent receptacle of *dark energy* as he used to get regular supply of it from the *Dark Goddess Kali*. So, whenever he wished, he could draw *dark energy* from Sri Chaitanya and take his *subtle* form and appeared as Chaitanya Dev himself to his devotees and disciples.

Instance 2

Once Sri Sri Ramakrishna had gone to Nabadwip to visit Sri Chaitanya's birthplace. He had his nephew Hriday with him. They toured the whole of Nabadwip but Thakur was not satisfied at all as he could not find any sign that Sri Gouranga was born there. If it were Sri Gouranga's birthplace, there would be *Hari Nam* sung there all the time, but no such vibrations were felt. When they had stepped on to the boat for their return journey, suddenly Thakur got the sight of two fair-skinned most handsome boys with an *aura* encircling their heads moving fast towards him on the sky above. The moment he saw them, he shouted: "They are coming! Gour-Nitai! Gour-Nitai are coming!" They approached him very fast and entered straight into his body. Thakur lost his consciousness; Hriday held him tightly, otherwise he would have fallen into the river water. On regaining his senses, Thakur was happy that he could get a concrete proof that the place was really the one where Bhagawan Sri Krishna Chaitanya was born centuries ago.

There was another strange revelation. Thakur could visualise, using his *Third Eye*, that his devotees Balaram Basu and Master Masai being present amongst the devotees of Sri Chaitanya Dev. He could thus understand their real past identities and that they had been close to him from their past lives.

Instance 3

Once Thakur and Hriday had gone to visit the Colootola Harisabha. Thakur had been invited there to listen to the special reading session on Srimad Bhagavad.

In that session, there was a special seat created for Bhagawan Sri Krishna Chaitanya. The reader of Srimad Bhagavad was reading out as if to Chaitanya Dev himself. While listening to the sacred reading, Ramakrishna entered into a special *bhava* and went straight to the special seat made for Chaitanya Dev, stood on it and lost consciousness. His face started glowing with a divine *aura*, and brimming with authentic love he raised one finger upwards as if Sri Gouranga himself had descended from up above. The present devotees were also overwhelmed and they all started chanting the name of Lord Hari. Thakur joined the devotee crowd and started dancing with them. The devotees got so motivated that the *Hari Nam* and the dance continued for long.

The orthodox Vaishnavas heard about this incident and they did not like it at all. Bhagawan Das Babaji of Kalna, a staunch Vaishnav, when he heard about this incident, he was very upset and he started criticising Thakur vehemently.

However, a few weeks after this incident, Thakur, along with Mathur Babu and Hriday went to Nabadwip via Kalna. As the boat reached to town Kalna, they came out for a tour of the Kalna town. When they reached the ashram of Bhagawan Das Babaji, Thakur covered himself up with a scarf and followed Hriday to enter the ashram. However, his vibrations were so highly spiritual that Bhagawan Das Babaji could feel it as he said: "I can feel the presence of some great soul in my ashram."

Bhagawan Das, like a typical Vaishnav, was counting the beads in the name of Bhagawan Hari at that time and when Hriday asked him why he being such a senior Krishna devotee was still counting beads and doing *japam*, his reply was most prompt. He said: "This practice may not be necessary for me. But I have to do it for teaching the masses." Thakur uncovered himself and said: "What? You are so proud? You are going to teach the masses? Who are you to teach them? It is He who has created them would teach them." While talking about the Supreme Creator, Thakur lost his senses. His real 'self' was exposed. Babaji, when he heard that this man was none else than Sri Ramakrishna who had stood on Sri Chaitanya Mahaprabhu's *asana* at the Colootola Harisabha, he started regretting and sought Thakur's forgiveness again and again. He asked as to how can he be free from what mistake he had committed. When he heard from Hriday that Thakur does not consider any mistake as a sin and does not take it so seriously, Babaji went round him seven times and touched his feet. When Mathur came back from outside looking for Thakur, Babaji said that he was not just a *Mahapurush*; he was *Mahaprabhu.* He considered himself very fortunate that he had met Thakur on that day.

Mathur had donated ten rupees to Babaji's ashram initially; but on Thakur's insistence, he donated ninety rupees more. Bhagawan Das was so happy!

Instance 4

Once Thakur Ramakrishna came to Sihor from Kamarpukur. And, there he had a *vision* of Sri Chaitanya Mahaprabhu. The local villagers had not known much about Sri Gouranga earlier. Now, when Ramakrishna started chanting *Hare Krishna* and dancing, the villagers also got into the mood and joined him in the dance. They started traversing the whole village chanting, singing and dancing along with Sri Ramakrishna. Thakur got into his *mahabhava* and his fair skinned body started glowing like gold – he was looking like Sri Gouranga Mahaprabhu. Like him, Thakur started tolling on the floor and his soft skin was getting cuts and bruises. Nobody could stop him and, finally, his nephew Hriday had to intervene. With the help of Hriday, Thakur distributed necklaces made of *tulsi* beads to all. Totally charged with love and happiness everyone left. Only one person, Nafar Bandyopadhyay stayed on. He was in a meditative mood. Nafar Babu used to worship Sri Krishna and he had a *vision* of Sri Krishna in Thakur Ramkrishna.

he feet of Thakur – got it blessed by him
s still in a *trance*.

sforming Darkness into Light

as to how Sri Sri Ramakrishna used to
women who had fallen into darkness.

Instance 1

Once, during his visit to the Star Theatre, the famous poet and playwright Girish Chandra Ghosh had called all his actresses and female dancers to meet the Paramhansa. These women who used to live in darkness mustered courage and confidence to meet Thakur face to face. The famous Nati Vinodini was amongst them. She prostrated in front of Thakur when he started singing a devotional song. Subsequently, each of the women followed the Nati. Ramakrishna blessed them profusely by saying: "You are providing happiness to people by acting, singing, and dancing. That is a great way to serve God. Do it with your whole heart and soul."

Thakur was most impressed with the acting of Nati Vinodini in the play "Sri Chaitanya". He went into a high mood and, at the end of the play, he met the Nati and gave her the *mantra*: "Hari Guru, Guru Hari". The woman who had fallen and had lived in darkness, with the golden touch of Thakur, got totally turned her into an ultra-pious lady.

Instance 2

Once Ramakrishna was visiting his devotee Ram Chandra Dutta. Getting the news of Thakur's visit, one ugly-looking prostitute came to get his blessings. She started singing a song, sitting outside the room where Ramakrishna was present. Hearing the song, Thakur went into a deep trance after he came out from the room and told the woman in a semi-conscious tone: "You have poured your heart into your song. Please keep singing!" The fallen woman fell on his feet and she felt as if she has got purified for the rest of her life.

Instance 3

Her real name was 'Chapala Sundari Devi' but people used
her 'Kalur Ma'. As she had no offspring of her own, she had ad
a boy by the name of Kalidas. She came from a brahmin family a
her father got her married to an elderly brahmin who did not survive for long. She got allured by the son of a rich landlord and, eventually, she was living in the prostitute quarters of Mechua Bazar in North Calcutta. In her entirely dark life, the only ray of light was Thakur Ramakrishna whom she would visit every day in Dakshineswar to get his blessings. Even extreme inclement weather conditions could not dissuade her from keeping up this habit. She had told her adopted son Kalidas to chant the name of 'Ramakrishna' three times at her last moment of passage to after-life. It is said that his son had followed this wish of hers.

Instance 4

People used to call 'Neerada Moni Dasi' as 'Neeru Thako'. She used to work part-time in many houses in Dakshineswar to help the householder women in various ways. In her youth, she used to play in the role of a *sakhi* in local theatre. Be it summer, monsoon, winter or spring, she used to take her bath very early in The Ganges, collect some holy water and sprinkle it in front of the room where Thakur used to stay. She used to say that the floor in front of Thakur's room was very sacred as it used to have his footfalls all the time. She used to sprinkle water and then collect it again. She used to consider Ramakrishna as God and would feel blessed by collecting the slime from the front of his room.

Instance 5

The first few years of the youth of Padma Rani Devi were spent in dark holes. Later on, she had dedicated herself to Thakur Ramakrishna. She had earned a lot of fame by singing *kirtans*. During her old age, she used to sing to herself, sitting in the veranda just outside Thakur's room.

Actually, one night she witnessed Ramakrishna's bright face in her dream. The very next day, she arrived at Dakshineswar to meet Thakur and take his blessings. On meeting her, Thakur told her to continue singing. He said: "Why would say: "Why should let others enjoy your body. That is entirely yours – the outer case and the inner parts. You keep singing.....devotional songs of Krishna.....devotional songs of Goddess Kali. But you must sing by putting all your heart and soul into it. All your mental pains and agonies must get expressed through your songs. You'll see, how miraculously you get relief from your sufferings."

She left her earlier wretched life and took lessons in *kirtan* singing. She started living at Kamarhati. She passed away during a singing trip outside her home.

Instance 6

Rai Kishori Dasi was commonly known as 'Ratir Ma'. She spent her youth as a prostitute but, later on, got reformed and started following a religious path. Most likely, it was after she had met Sri Sri Ramakrishna at Dakshineswar where she was a local resident.

Instance 7

Sarat Kumari (popularly known as Swari Buri). She used to sell milk, home to home, in the Dakhshineswar area. She used to buy the milk and distribute it in different fixed homes. She had also been blessed by Thakur.

Instance 8

Sushila Devi had a daughter by the name of Manda. So, she was called as 'Mandar Ma'. She used to work as a maid in the house of the Niyogis in Dakshineswar. People say that, in her youth, she used to sell her body; but later, she turned into a very pious and kind-hearted woman. That is the reason why everyone in the Dakshineswar village used to love her. And, Ramakrishna was behind this turnaround of hers. She used to say: "Ramakrishna is no less than God. He has the body of a God. And, his talks are not just words – they are gems.

Whatever he used to say would come true. I do not know what would have happened to me had I not got his blessings. Ma Sarada was also like a Goddess. I was too scared to go near Thakur and would worship him from a distance. That was not the case with Ma Sarada. She used to talk so much and so nicely with me. One day, I had told Ma Sarada about my wish to touch the feet of Thakur and she had assured me that it will certainly happen when the time came."

One day, when Mandar Ma was with Ma Sarada, they found Thakur was coming from the Panchabati side. Sri Sri Ma told Ramakrishna about Mandar Ma's wish. Paramhansa displayed a sweet smile, took her *pranam* and blessed her profusely. The woman had touched Thakur's feet too lightly lest she would hurt him. However, nothing had gone wrong and everything went off so well.

Instance 9

The granddaughter of Naba Kumar Chattopadhyay, a resident of Dakshineswar, was Tara Dasi Devi. She became a widow at the age of eight only. Naba Kumar, who was very close to Thakur, was very much concerned about the girl. Thakur assured him that whatever had happened must have been good for the girl. Thakur said that Tara was born with a slice of *Devi Mahamaya*, so she was not destined to undergo the sufferings of a householder's life. Thakur had blessed her by saying that she will certainly develop *bhakti bhava* soon. Living at her father's house, she started studying sacred texts, some of which she had learnt by heart. She also used to cook very well and items prepared by her were most favourite of Thakur. She breathed her last at the age of 83. Just before she passed away, she had told her relatives who were present to chant Sri Sri Ramakrishna's name to her.

Instance 10

One day, Thakur was inside the temple of Mother Bhavatarini, visualising the different *rupas* of the Goddess. He could visualise that the *dark goddess* was omnipresent. Suddenly, he could see the presence of a woman behind the deity's image. Then he thought that it must have been an illusion and nothing else. As he came out of the temple and was walking up to his room, he could find a well-ornamented woman approaching towards him and she resembled exactly the lady whom he had seen behind the image in the temple. As she tried to reach his feet to take her blessing, he refused by saying: "How can I allow you to touch my feet as I saw you inside the temple beside the Goddess? I saw you in the form of my mother!" Hearing her being addressed as 'mother', tears started rolling down her cheeks.

This was Ramani, the prostitute. Ramakrishna ignored her prostitute role and visualised the 'mother' inside her.

Ramakrishna never used to discriminate between *whiteness* and *darkness*. He used to believe that inside anyone who had a *dark* past, whether it is a man or a woman, there is dormant *dark energy*. Ramakrishna had the power to stimulate it to become active and utilised for productive purposes. There are so many such examples. I have shared only a few.

How Sri Sri Ramakrishna Transformed Girish Chandra Ghosh

Girish used to feel that his life was very much like the pungent-smelling garlic; whichever container it will be kept, its pungent smell will never disappear. He had once asked the *Paramhansa*, most desperately: "How the pungent smell will go?" Thakur had answered: "If you ignite the container with flame, the disturbing smell will vanish".

On another occasion, when he was cursing himself as a 'sinner', Sri Ramakrishna consoled him by saying: "When light comes, darkness accumulated over a thousand years just disappear in less than a second. Likewise, whenever one gets God's grace, one develops unstinted faith in his powers, all sins start vanishing in a minute's time".

Girish used to notice how the devotees were serving Thakur and he used to think that if Thakur had been born into his family as his son, he will take full care of him as his own offspring.

One day, Thakur had gone to witness one of Girish's popular plays. As he was coming out of the hall after eating fresh savouries arranged by Girish, fully drunk Girish started nagging to Ramakrishna: "Thakur, promise me that you'll be born as my son.....promise me." Thakur responded: "My father was a most pious brahmin, why should I be your son?" This made Girish furious. He started abusing Thakur right and left. This made the devotees present most upset and asked Ramakrishna not to go near such a scoundrel.

On the next day, there was discussion on the same topic in Dakshineswar. Ramakrishna was listening to the discussion, most quietly, without any comment. Suddenly, Thakur's devotee Ram Chandra Dutta stepped in and Thakur asked him: "Ram, what do you think?" Ram Babu replied: "Thakur, the poisonous Kaliya snake had told Bhagawan Sri Krishna – where would I find the nectar which will take away all my poison. Girish Babu is in a similar situation. Where would he get the nectar which will wash away all his alcohol?"

Thakur said: "Ram, you have brought your vehicle, isn't it? Let us go to Girish in your vehicle." On the other side, after Girish's hangover had cleared off, he could realise what sin he had committed and, most regretfully, he had given up consuming any food. Just at that time Thakur entered by saying: "I've come as God wanted me to come." Girish fell on his feet and started sobbing: "if you had not come today, I'd have thought that you have not transcended beyond the level of discriminating between praise and abuse – you've not earned the right to be called *Paramhansa*. You'll not be able to cheat me any longer. I'm not going to leave you. Please promise me that you'll take my burden, you'll take my whole responsibility. I cannot carry my own burden any more. You'll have to rescue me from the *black hole*."

In the close company of Thakur Ramakrishna, he entered into a totally new phase of life. During his last days, he used to say: "If I had known earlier that there was such a huge receptacle available to keep my sins, then I'd have committed more sins." Ramakrishna *Paramhansa* was indeed a very big *black hole* who would suck all the sins of all the sinners that he would come across.

One night, Girish and his two friends, totally drunk, were going to prostitute quarters. Suddenly he had a very strong wish to meet Thakur. They turned the vehicle and went straight to him. The time was a little before midnight. Thakur left his bed, held Girish by his two hands and was overwhelmed with joy. He started singing and dancing without being conscious of whether he had clothes on or not. Girish had a wonderful feeling!! He thought no kin, not even the paid professional prostitutes, will entertain him in such a drunken mood. They will keep the door shut not allowing him to enter; and start cursing and abusing. So, he felt most strongly, that Ramakrishna's door will always be open for such people who are unacceptable in the society.

Girish had expressed his such feeling in front of everyone that Thakur was really God incarnate. He was Sri Krishna Chaitanya himself who had descended to rescue people like Jagai Madhai from dangerously *negative black holes* and give the shelter in his deeper and wider *positive black hole.*

So, during the extreme winter of his life, Girish composed eulogising Thakur:

"You are the receptacle full of pure love –
always totally expressed
unaffected by pleasure or pain, happiness or grief
totally wise is your personality and presence
Your door is always open for those who are found
unacceptable by their kin, the drunkards,
the lecherous, those having loose characters
and kept outside their close reach.
You take them close to your heart!!"

(Composed in Bengali by Girish Chandra Ghosh; adapted and translated into English by the author)

Bhagawan Sri Krishna Chaitanya and Avatar Sri Sri Ramakrishna had many things in common – one most remarkable amongst those were the presence of most powerful *positive black hole* in their personality which would rescue sinners from the deep dungeons of *negative black holes* and not only provide them shelter but with a three hundred and sixty degree turn in their personalities.

Sri Sri Ramakrishna's tolerance for different religions is very well-known. One striking example is his interest in Islam. On one side of the Dakshineswar temple, there was a Muslim burial ground and Ramakrishna had genuinely felt the Supreme Goddess had wished the temple to be a meeting place of all religions. So, Ramakrishna started his training in Islam by choosing one Gobinda Roy as his Guru. Gobinda used to visit Dakshineswar regularly. He would sit under the shady trees in the Panchabati area and spend some time most peacefully. Hindus and Muslims – all were equally welcome in the Dakshineswar Kalibari campus.

Thakur used to say: "Whenever you will meet people, love them all, do not discriminate. Try to be one with them. Study the nature and character of everyone and shower your love indiscriminately. Then go to your own house and share your peace and happiness with everyone."

A Religious Shrine: A Black Hole

A religious shrine – a temple, a church, a synagogue, a mosque, a gurdwara could also serve as a *black hole* as many people go there for their confessions, seeking forgiveness from the supreme power and authority.

Let me share a beautiful devotional song (originally in Bengali, translated by me in English):

> "Give me a little space
> to sit in the temple of the Supreme Mother
> to sit in the temple of the Supreme Mother!
>
> I am an unwanted person
> I am an unwanted person
> I am an unwanted person
> I have a history of many misdeeds.
>
> Give me a little space
> to sit in the temple of the Supreme Mother!

I will remain behind everyone
And only call the Supreme Mother
quietly in my mind!
If I'm disliked by anyone
punish me as much as you like.

Give me a little space
to sit in the temple of the Supreme Mother!
I am an unwanted person
I have a history of many misdeeds.

Give me a little space
to sit in the temple of the Supreme Mother!

Don't you think that I will
appear suddenly in front
to touch the divine feet of the Supreme Mother!
I will only watch from a distance
and bathe her feet with my tears!

Only when you will perform the *arati*
and lift and hold the lamp in your hand
please allow me to witness
the divine smile of the Supreme Mother
the divine smile of the Supreme Mother!

Give me a little space
to sit in the temple of the Supreme Mother
I am an unwanted person
I have a history of many misdeeds.

(Lyric: Pulak Bandyopadhyay)

The poet is offering himself to enter into the *black hole* of the shrine, looking for a little opportunity.

Any religious shrine is such a sacred place that it sucks all the past misdeeds and sins of those who visit the place and have their *prasads* there.

Every day, many beggars and destitutes used to visit the Dakshineswar temple to have *prasad.* After eating, they never used to take the banana leaves on which *prasad* used to be served after their eating, dump those in the Ganges River and clean up the place. Ramakrishna used to do that job every day most happily, as he had no discriminatory feeling. Possibly, he used to feel that it was not a heinous act which he was performing; on the contrary, all the negativity left by the beggar guests had been devoured by the sacred place and replaced by purity and virtue.

Thakur used to say: "Those who visit the temple are mostly devotees (*bhaktas*). They have no religion, class or caste. Devotion purifies the body, mind and soul." (References 9–15)

Sri Sri Ramakrishna and His *White Hole* Behaviour

In the celestial galaxies, there are *white holes* that behave in an exactly reverse way of *black holes. Black holes* consume and suck in, *white holes* eject, spit out.

Once Sri Sri Ramakrishna was visiting Surendra's house. Surendra was a well-to-do person. In the drawing room on the first floor of Surendra's house, many devotees had assembled. Local neighbours like Mahendra Goswami and Bholanath Pal were also present. There were a few members of the Brahmo Samaj including Trailokya Sanyal. An expensive carpet was spread out on the floor and a side pillow was kept for Thakur Ramakrishna's use. Surendra requested Thakur to sit on the expensive carpet. Thakur rejected the idea, behaving like a *white hole* and sat on the plain mat which had been spread out for all common people to sit on.

Surendra brought, in his own hand, an expensive garland which he wanted Thakur to put on. Once again Thakur behaved like a *white hole* and rejected the idea. And, thereafter, he took the garland and threw it away to a distance. Surendra was very upset as he had spent a lot of money for that garland. He started shedding tears and said: "I can realise my fault now. I have a rich man's big ego. God does not care about wealth. I don't feel like living now." Tears started flowing down his cheeks. That melted Thakur. He lifted the garland that he had thrown away a little while earlier. He put it on. Trailokya started singing and Thakur started dancing. Once the singing and dancing stopped, Thakur asked Surendra: "Are you not going to feed me anything?" This golden touch transformed Surendra into a man of gold.

A few months later, one disciple of Swami Vivekananda had wished to offer *bhog* to Thakur. Surendra said he will make all arrangements. He got up very early, went to the market, purchased everything. However, while returning he did not allow the earthen container of sweet curd to be carried in the horse-drawn carriage lest the thickness and density of the curd get spoilt with the vibrations of the carriage moving. Instead, he carried it himself and covered all the distance on foot. Swamiji, with moist eyes, remarked to his disciple: "Can you see? Didn't I tell you those whom Thakur has touched once have turned into gold. Here is one example right in front of our eyes."

How a *White Hole* was Turned into a *Black Hole*

A young householder devotee used to visit Sri Sri Ramakrishna regularly, every Saturday, from Konnagar. He was very favourite of everyone in his family which had made him over-sentimental and that is why he became a little upset when he got exposed to anybody else's praise.

On one Saturday, when he was in Dakshineswar, Thakur was praising, very highly, Surendra Nath Mitra's devotion in front of everyone. Except for that young man, everyone else had known and was familiar with Surendra Nath, so they were all very pleased. It was silly for him that he got emotionally hurt. He felt unloved and uncared for. He thought Thakur loved Surendra much more than him. So, from next Saturday, he gave up visiting Dakshineswar totally. It was a *white hole* behaviour on his part. If anybody asked him, he would say: "Let the *Paramhansa* stay with his beloved ones; I have nothing to do with him".

His absence for a few weeks did not escape Thakur's notice. Thakur enquired about him: where had he disappeared and why? He sent one of the young man's relatives to bring him around. Unfortunately, neither did the young man visit Dakshineswar nor did he allow his relative to return to Dakshineswar to report to Thakur about him. He, however, sent a message that he would certainly visit once he considered himself really devoted to Thakur. Indirectly, he wanted to convey that let Thakur remain with those who, he felt, were really devoted to him. However, inside he was suffering too much. He was missing the vibrations of *Paramhansa.*

The young man used to go for his bath to the Holy River Ganges. This was an old habit of his. One day, a strange thing happened. One early morning, he was worshipping the Sun God having his body dipped in neck-deep water, suddenly when he opened his eyes, he found a boat came in his direction very fast and stopped almost near him. He was about to say something to the boatman when he discovered Thakur's dedicated devotee Balaram Basu was standing on the boat. Taken a little aback, the young man said: "How fortunate I am that I had *darshan* of a great devotee of Thakur so early in the morning."

Balaram Babu answered most promptly: "It is not only the devotee, Thakur himself has come to enquire why are you not visiting Dakshineswar".

Hearing this, when the young man looked around, he found Thakur himself standing on one side of the boat – in a half-trance with tears rolling down his cheeks. In deep regret, he fell on the feet of Thakur and started crying. God himself has come down to take the emotionally upset and sensitive devotee into his deep embrace. This act of Thakur was good enough to transform the *white hole* devotee into a *black hole* one. The name of this young man was Manomohan.

References

[1] Swami Chetanananda, *Sri Ramakrishner Sannidhye* (In Bengali), Kolkata: Udbodhan, 1st Edition, 20th Impression, 2022, p. 2, pp. 12–16.

[2] "What is Pran Pratistha and why the Shankaracharyas are not attending it?" *TOI Lifestyle Desk, TimesofIndia.com* 15th January 2024.

[3] William Clark, "Is my Mother Shyama Black? A Song of Kamalakanta"

Kali Bhakti, An Offering for Our Divine Mother, kalibhakti.com, 9th March 2019.

[4] Hope Reese, "How a Bit of Awe Can Improve Your Health", *The New York Times*, 3rd January 2023.

[5] Paul Wright, MD, "The neuroscience and health benefits of experiencing awe and wonder", *Nuvance Health*, 8th September 2024.

[6] Elise Herman, MD, "The Benefits of Awe-inspiring Experiences for Kids", *KVH (Kittitas Valley Healthcare)*, 7th September 2023.

[7] "Dacher Keltner: Why Awe Is Such an Important Emotion", Video Presentation on YouTube, Greater Good Science Center, UC Berkeley.

[8] Suman Bhattacharya, *Dui Avatar: Sri Chaitanya o Sri Ramakrishna* (In Bengali), Kolkata: Girija Library, 2020, pp. 59–61, pp. 66–67, pp. 71–73, p. 75, p. 79, pp. 88–92, pp. 95–97.

[9] "Oxytocin" – *Wikipedia.*

[10] Paul J. Zak, *The Moral Molecule: How Trust Works*, New York: Plume (The Penguin Group), 2013.

[11] Swami Chetanananda, *Sri Ramakrishner Sannidhye*, (In Bengali) Kolkata: Udbodhan Karjalaya, 20th Impression, 2022, pp. 14–15.

[12] "What If a White Hole and a Black Hole Collided?" Video Presentation on YouTube, 'What If' Channel.

[13] "What Happens When a White Hole and a Black Hole Collide?" Video Presentation on YouTube; The Action Lab Channel.

[14] Suman Bhattacharya, *Dui Avatar: Sri Chaitanya O Sri Ramakrishna* (In Bengali), Kolkata: Girija Library, 2020, pp. 76–77, pp. 83-84, pp. 176–184.

[15] "Amay Ektu Jayga Dao Lyrics", amarkobita4u.com/2C

Epilogue

At the end, let me tell you that I am neither a *Shakta* nor a *Vaishnava*. Being a Hindu 'brahmin', I believe in *Brahma* – the 'Universal Energy' and where it resides – the *Brahmanda* – the 'Universe' where the souls from all religions ultimately go, meet and assemble, irrespective of whether Hindu, or Muslim, Christian, Jewish, Buddhist, Sikh or Zoroastrian, adding to the *dark energy* of the space.

I echo with the Bangladeshi Muslim singer-songwriter-composer-instrumentalist *Farzana Wahid Shayan*:

> "I mingle with the Hindus – some of them are my aunts
> on my mother's and my father's –
> on both sides!
> I visit the homes of Christians, I am neither biased
> nor against any religion
> I have plucked fragrant flowers from all religions having
> forgotten the thorny experiences
> I am not stuck anywhere due to any false prejudice
> I pray to the Supreme for everyone!!"

I have studied Sri Krishna Chaitanya and Sri Sri Ramakrishna to explore if there was any *Science* in the *Religious Art* that they had practised and preached; and, whatever I have found extraordinary in them but scientifically justified and explicable, I try to follow in my own life and highlight those for my readers to follow in their lives!!

APPENDIX I

The Science of Dark Energetics

The *Vaishnava* faith, as one can very clearly see, is divided into two distinctly different categories. The first one, if I am allowed to relate it to the subtle *yogic chakras*, practised by the *Sahajiya Vaishnavas*, attaches their theme to the three lower *chakras* of the body, starting from the tail end of the spine – in this sequence, *muladhara* (the 'Root'), *swadhisthana* (the 'Sacral'), and *manipura* (the 'Solar Plexus'). In the *tantric* outlook, this can arise from the *Poshu Bhava* (Pre-human, primeval) and/or the *Naro* or *Veera Bhava* (Human, Hunter-gatherer, Farmer).

Sahajiya, a form of Hindu *Tantric Vaishnavism* – flourished from the 16th to the 18th century, believes that there is an innate or primordial condition (the *Sahaja*) present in everyone – the urge for pro-creation, transmission of the *genes*. In order this process to be carried out, you need a member of the opposite sex. This is the natural propensity of *Mother Nature* in every individual – whether it be a male or a female. Each of us has the *Universe* (*Brahmanda*) in our body (*Deha Bhanda*) with that power and potential. The romance between Krishna and Radha, the *Sahajiyas* sought to experience through the physical reenactment in the *tantric* way by making use of sexual intercourse during the menstruation of the female partner without ejaculation, instead mixing the semen with the menstrual blood and moving it upward. This was a very special *sadhana* that required some expert guidance followed by a period of practice. Krishna and Radha were thus regarded as absolutely normal human beings – a male and a female having *sahajiya* (innate, normal) urges for sensory gratification, comparable to the Adam and Eve of Christianity, where the 'forbidden fruit' symbolised 'prevention of ejaculation'. The *Sahajiya Vaishnav* philosophy and practices were greatly influenced by the Bengali Buddhist *tantric* tradition that was also known as *Sahajiya* which made use of *tantric* sexuality.

Sahajiya Vaishnavism thrived in the pre-Chaitanya era and it used to get propagated through beautiful poetry composed by a number of talented poets. One sample is given below.

A *sahajiya* poem of *Vidyapati* (1352?? – 1448??), rendered into English by David R. Kinsley (1975) says:

> "As I near the bed, he smiles and gazes,
> Flower-arrows fill the world.
> The sport of love, its glow and luxuries are indescribable, O friend,
> And when I yield myself, his joy is endless.
>
> Freeing my skirt, he snatches at my garland.
> My downcast mind is freed of frontiers.
> Though my life is held in the net of his love,
> He drinks my lips.
> With heart so thrilled, he takes my clothes away
> I lose my body at his touch and long to check
> But grunt his love.
> Says Vidyapati: Sweet as honey is the talk of a girl in love."

Sahajiyas concentrate on the 'control' of the body's energies ('breath', 'sperms' and 'ova') which is also prevalent in some of the practices of the Bauls and Fakirs.

Although the *Sahajiya* concepts and practices still live, insignificantly, in some of the Hindu Bauls of Bengal and Bangladesh, *Vaishnavism* in its theory and practice has been greatly changed as we find it today in *Gaudiya Vaishnavism*, introduced by Mahaprabhu Sri Krishna Chaitanya where the *erotic* (*sringara*) flavour of devotion has been eliminated to give it a more divine flavour (*divya bhava*) relating it to the *chakras* higher than the lowest three – the *anahata* (heart), the *visuddhi* (throat) and the *ajna* ('third eye') *chakras*. Chaitanya had uplifted the whole movement to a much higher plane which involved transaction of *dark energy* – its collection from the *Dark God Krishna* and its expenditure and sharing with others by performing *nam sankirtan* with dancing in a typical *Vaishnava* style.

Most Recent Findings About *Dark Energy*

Recent observations on supermassive *black holes* at the centre of galaxies point to a likely source of *Dark Energy*, the 'missing' 68–70% of the Universe. The study was conducted by a team of 17 researchers in nine countries, led by the University of Hawaii. The team included scientists from the Imperial College, London and STFC Space – UKRI – Rutherford Appleton Laboratory. The work is published in the journals *The Astrophysical Journal* and *The Astrophysical Journal Letters.* The study was led by Duncan Farrah of the University of Hawaii who stated in conclusion: "*Black holes* in Einstein's 'Theory of Gravity' are the *Dark Energy*". (References 1–3)

Why Fair-skinned Sri Radhika was Attracted Towards the Dark God Krishna

I have not looked much into Vaishnava literature; however, whatever I have studied moderatey, I have studied absolutely thoroughly. And, I have not come across any explanation which is worthy of ready acceptance by a veteran human scientist like me of why Sri Radhika was attracted towards Bhagawan Krishna. Was it because of his lineage? Was it because of his innocent charm? Was it because of his mesmerising playing of the flute? Or was it because of his physical constitution?

After pondering on the matter for hours and days, I have come to a definite conclusion which, to my mind, is the only scientific explanation.

Dark Energy (the term coined by the University of Chicago astrophysicist Michael Turner in 1998) is surrounded by its own magnetic field which attracts, *most strongly*, those who have a strong *Dark Energy Hunger. 'Dark Energy'* represents deep, unconditional love and a trusting bonded relationship for which the neurochemical is *Oxytocin* (*O*) secreted from the brain's Pituitary 'Glands'. Sri Radhika (we can only speculate as we can't question her as is done in a research study or survey) had a very strong *Oxytocin* hunger because of her possible *Oxytocin* deprivation during her childhood and growing years. So, when she met Krishna for the first time, the *dark youth* attracted her immediately like a magnet. In fact, Lord Krishna had descended on earth as Sri Krishna Chaitanya with a *Radha Bhava* in the male body to find out how Sri Radhika felt and used to feel in the absence of the physical proximity of Krishna.

Radha's strong fancy for *dark* colour is expressed beautifully in a verse by the famed poet Chandidas in the pre-Chaitanya Bengal (Reference 8, p.37, translation from Bengali – mine):

> "When I pour *dark* water from the pitcher, I shudder
> As the memory of the *dark* youth flash on my mind's mirror
> I see his *dark* splendour in my sleep and also in my dreams
> I don't let my *dark* hair become loose and I do not use collyrium in my eyes
> Lest I remember him and suffer from anxiety due to separation from my *dark* lover!!"

Another paragraph I'm quoting from Jibendu Roy (Reference 8, p.60 & p.110) which expresses, metaphorically, Radhika's craving for the *dark energy* (translation from Bengali – mine):

> "Radhika is tormented by acute heartache. She sits alone in desolate places and does not respond to anybody's call. She gets lost by looking at the dark clouds passing by, high in the sky, resembling her most beloved *Dark God.* She looks on without changing her sight anywhere. She has no appetite; she has lost all interest in the consumption of food. Earlier she used to put on deep bluish dresses, but now she has given it up, losing all interest. She unlocks her plait, takes her dark black hair in her hand and looks at it ceaselessly, as if she has found her beloved there. She again lifts her head from the locks of hair and looks at the dark clouds passing, and indulges in self-talk. Nobody can make out what she says. She looks at the deep blue hue in the neck of a peacock dancing nearby."

Most, amazingly, the same intensity of 'separation anxiety' Sri Chaitanya Mahaprabhu had displayed in his life when he would brim with *Krishna (the 'Dark God') Consciousness* in his soul.

Oxytocin is the 'love-and-trust molecule' – *premarasa* in Sanskrit, whereas *Dopamine* is the quick-fix 'feel good molecule' – *'kamarasa'* in Sanskrit, which is released from the 'Reward Circuit' of the brain on any type of sensory gratification and fulfilment of any desire including for sexual satisfaction. The relationship between Radha and Krishna was *Oxytocin-centric* and not *Dopamine-centric* as some might mistakenly think.

Most interestingly, all classical verses in Vaishnava literature written by famous poets like Jayadeva, Chandidas and Vidyapati during the pre-Chaitanya era had shown the Radha-Krishna relationship more of a *dopaminergic* nature.

To quote Jayadeva from his poetic creation *Gita Govinda*:

> "O woman with desire, place on this patch of flower-strewn floor your lotus foot,
> And let your foot through beauty win,
> To me who am the Lord of All. O be attached, now always yours,
> O follow me, my little Radha."

It was Chaitanya who highlighted the importance of the *oxytocin*-based relationship between the two, to be followed in practice. His disciples around Vrindavan region, affirmed Radha as the "hladini shakti" ("energy of bliss") of Krishna, associating her with the Primordial Divine Mother, who was providing *Vatsalya Rasa* to the *Dark God.*

According to David Kinsley, a professor of Religious Studies, known for his studies on Hindu goddesses, the Radha-Krishna love story is a metaphor for a divine-human relationship, where Radha is the human devotee or soul who is frustrated with the past, obligations and social expectations, and the ideas she has inherited, who then longs for the real meaning, the true love, the divine (Krishna). The metaphoric Radha (soul) finds new liberation in learning more about Krishna, bonding in devotion, and with passion. Kinsley's observations fit very well with my idea of the *oxytocin*-based relationship between the two.

The Gaudiya tradition focuses upon *parakiya-rasa* as the highest form of love, wherein Radha and Krishna share thoughts even through separation as there is an invisible emotional bridge between the two. The love the *gopis* feel for Krishna is also described in this esoteric manner as the highest platform of spontaneous love of God, and not of a sexual nature. This reminds me of Professor Rupert Sheldrake's wonderful theory of *Morphic Resonance* although reductionist scientists regard his works as 'pseudo-scientific'.

Radha had once asked Krishna why he can't marry her. Prompt came the reply: "Marriage is a union of two souls. You and I are only one soul, how can I marry myself?" Did Krishna mean that their souls were united due to their *dark energy* content, having darkness of equal density which had merged them into each other with no perceptible difference in any respect? Did he mean that marriages take place for balancing of the souls when the energy quantity and quality are different and blending was necessary for a happy life for both. (Reference 4–12)

References

[1] "Vaishnava Sahajiya" – *Wikipedia.*

[2] David R. Kinsley *The sword and the flute: Kali and Krishna, dark visions of the terrible and the sublime in Hindu mythology*, California: University of California Press, 1975, pp. 48–49.

[3] Hayley Dunning, "Scientists find first evidence that black holes are the source of dark energy", *Imperial News*, 15th February 2023.

[4] "Dark Energy" – *Wikipedia.*

[5] "Dark Energy Explained" *UChicago News.*

[6] "Oxytocin" – *Wikipedia.*

[7] "Dopamine" – *Wikipedia.*

[8] Jibendu Ray, *Gaudiya Vaishnav Darshan – Pad O Padakar*, (In Bengali) Kolkata: Sahityasree, Refurbished Edition, 2023.

[9] David Kinsley, *Hindu Goddesses: ion of the Divine Feminine in the Hindu Religious Tradition,* Delhi: Motilal Banarasidass Publishers, Reprint, 2005.

[10] Guy L. Beck, Ed. *Alternative Krishnas: Regional and Vernacular Variations on a Hindu Deity,* Stony Brook: SUNY Press, 2006.

[11] Rupert Sheldrake, *A New Science of Life: The Hypothesis of Morphic Resonance,* Rochester, Vermont: Inner Traditions Bear and Company, Reprint Edition 1995.

[12] Rupert Sheldrake, *A New Science of Life,* Merrywalks: Stroud, Gloucestershire, UK. ICON Books, 2009.

APPENDIX II

Dark Energy and Its Healing Power

The reaction between the *dark energy* and the different kinds of matter contained in the universe is found to possibly have some power to rejuvenate many forms of lives in this cosmos. There are different kinds of energy, already being utilised and used for the treatment of different types of ailments and diseases. These include: X-ray, gamma ray, ultra-violet ray, beta ray, and rays used in radiation therapy, magnetic resonance imaging, computed tomography scanning, radioactive tracers, single photon emission computed tomography, and positron emission tomography.

In the earth's galaxy, gravity is the dominant force, so *dark energy* may have little influence although it is abundantly available in the universe in different forms. The ancient Indian sages had realised its potent power and had developed the concepts of *Dark Gods* [Lord Krishna, Lord Shiva (Shiva Linga as well as Neelakantha Shiva), Lord Rama] and a fierce *Dark Goddess* (Goddess Kali).

The Theory of Dimensions

Day-to-day, we live with 3D (three-dimensional) objects. Our own *Gross Body* is a 3D object. We have: height (or length), width (or breadth), and depth (or thickness). 3D is an entirely *physical* concept. According to Einstein's *Relativity*, the 4th dimension is 'Time'. All the stars and planets in the galaxies of the universe are 3D objects moving in a SPACE-TIME continuum. The 5th Dimension may be a *phantom* or *ghost dark energy*, which causes the expansion of the universe to accelerate quickly. So, the 5th Dimension is a state of pure potential and heightened vibration. It is a space of unconditional love, happiness, freedom, egoless-ness, and abundance. While up to the 4th Dimension is 'material', the 5th Dimension is 'spiritual'. While in the former, we seek 'pleasure' by earning the 'Feel Good Molecule' *Dopamine (D)* from the 'Reward Circuit' of our brain, latter is the zone of 'Sustained Happiness and Bliss' featuring the 'Trust Molecule' *Oxytocin (O)*, the 'Bliss Molecule' *Anandamide (ANA/AEA)* and the 'Spirit Molecule' *Di-Methyl-Tryptamine (DMT)* which, it has been proven through the cases of Sri Krishna Chaitanya and Sri Sri Ramakrishna – can be reached through total consciousness filled with *dark energy* – respectively Lord Krishna and Goddess Kali. Spiritual teachings see the 5D as our natural state of being as spiritual beings. As humans, we are inherently drawn to experiencing the 5th Dimension. This translates to our desire for love, happiness and fulfilment. It is seen as the ultimate goal – a state of oneness and connection with everything. Through spiritual practices, we can elevate our consciousness and ascend to this higher vibrational state.

Body States

Our *Gross Body* is a 3D concept as we have: height (length), width (breadth), and depth (thickness). This 3D body changes with the 4th D – 'time' as we age. We can postpone ageing to a limited extent by taking physical fitness exercises, regulated conscious breathing practices and following a planned controlled diet. The *Subtle Body* is primarily the *Soul*. It is also subjected to the ageing process, but we can keep it young and fresh – primarily by effective *DMN Management*. One sure-shot technique is to remain, most of the time, in the 'FLOW Brain State' ('FBS') – even while falling asleep and also in the 'Rapid Eye Movements' ('REM') ('dreaming') and 'Non-Rapid Eye Movements' ('NREM') states of sleep. This can also help to reduce your sleeping time.

If you can practice 'Effective Subtle Body Management' ('ESBM') or 'Effective Soul Management' ('ESM'), you can live a long, healthy, meaningful, productive life.

Journey Through the Dimensions

'Journey Through the Dimensions' is the process of *spiritual ascension*. Up to the stage of puberty or adolescence, the child should be guided to have a 4D existence – the 4th D being 'Effective Time Management'. Then, if necessary, a Mentor's (*Guru's*) guidance would be required to have an effective 5th D living and working, struggling to defeat the 'Six Enemies of the Mind' (*Sada Ripus*)and breaking free from the 'Eight Fetters' ('*Asta Pas*').

In the 5D state of consciousness, we experience a deep sense of peace and oneness with all of existence. We move beyond the illusion of separation and duality and live in a state of unconditional love and compassion. Life becomes less about *DOING* and more about *BEING*. (References 1 & 2)

References

[1] Koijam Manihar Singh and Kangujam Priyokumar Singh, "Whether dark energy can contribute to the treatment and healing of diseases", *Modern Physics Letters A*, 2019, Vol. 34, No. 32, 1950260.

[2] Anika Naneyshvili, "Unveiling the Mysteries of Multi-dimensional Reality – Exploring Beyond Our Everyday Experience (3D, 4D, 5D Dimensional Realities for Manifestation), 1st June 2024, anikaloveyoga.com